The Bridge Series

STORIES FROM MANY LANDS

THE BRIDGE SERIES

STORIES
FROM MANY LANDS

Edited by
G. C. Thornley, M.A. Ph.D.

Illustrated by
Victor J. Bertoglio

LONGMAN

LONGMAN GROUP LIMITED
London

*Associated companies, branches and representatives
throughout the world*

© Longman Group Ltd 1964

*First published *1964
New impressions *1964; *1965; *1966 (twice);
*1967; *1968; *1969 (twice);
*1970 (twice); *1971;
*1972; *1974 (twice) ; *1975*

ISBN 0 582 53025 3

*Printed in Hong Kong by
Peninsula Press Ltd*

The Bridge Series

The *Bridge Series* is intended for students of English as a second or foreign language who have progressed beyond the elementary graded readers and the *Longman Simplified English Series* but are not yet sufficiently advanced to read works of literature in their original form.

The books in the *Bridge Series* are moderately simplified in vocabulary and often slightly reduced in length, but with little change in syntax. The purpose of the texts is to give practice in understanding fairly advanced sentence patterns and to help in the appreciation of English style. We hope that they will prove enjoyable to read for their own sake and that they will at the same time help students to reach the final objective of reading original works of literature in English with full understanding and appreciation.

Technical Note

The vocabulary of the *Simplified English Series* is the 2,000 words of the *General Service List (Interim Report on Vocabulary Selection)* and there is a degree of structure control. In the *Bridge Series* words outside the commonest 7,000 (in Thorndike and Lorge: *A Teacher's Handbook of* 30,000 *Words*, Columbia University, 1944) have usually been replaced by commoner and more generally useful words. Words used which are outside the first 3,000 of the list are explained in a glossary and are so distributed throughout the book that they do not occur at a greater density than 25 per running 1,000 words.

Acknowledgements

WE are grateful to the following for permission to include adaptations from copyright material :

The Educational Book Co. Ltd., London for the following stories from *The Masterpiece Library of Short Stories: The Rustic Cobbler* by E. Blasco, *The Cup of Tea* by A. Botelho, *The Chameleon* by A. Chekhov, *At the Palace of Justice* by A. Daudet, *The Expression* by J. Francés, *Boleslov* by M. Gorky, *The Tomb of Ali-Bellus* by V. B. Ibañez, *A Clump of Lilac* by A. Kuprin, *Ziré Buzette* by M. des Ombriaux, *The Cobbler Blondeau* by B. des Periers and *The Hoop* by F. Sologub; Eyre & Spottiswoode Ltd. and Charles E. Tuttle Co. for *The House of a Black Dog* by Sato Haruo from *Modern Japanese Stories;* the Estate of the late J. Jefferson Farjeon for *Waiting for the Police;* George G. Harrap & Co. Ltd. for *The Orderly* by E. de Amicis, *Mirrors* by M. Bontempelli and *The Beast* by J. Wassermann from *Great Stories of all Nations;* T. Werner Laurie Ltd. for *One or the Other* by R. Croft-Cooke from *A Football for the Brigadier and Other Stories;* and Penguin Books Ltd. for *The Piece of String* by Guy de Maupassant, translated by H. N. P. Sloman.

We have been unable to trace the copyright owners in: *When the Sun Went Down* by Henry Lawson; *The Accursed House* by Emile Gaboriau which appeared in the *Strand Magazine;* and *The Stub-book* by Pedro de Alarcon and *An Andalusian Duel* by Estébanez Calderón both published by the Walter Scott Publishing Co. Ltd., and should welcome any information which would enable us to do so.

Contents

When the Sun Went Down

HENRY LAWSON

Henry Lawson (1867–1922) was a true Australian, whose writing has a direct appeal to the understanding and sympathy of the reader. *When the Sun Went Down* is a short story about a quarrel between two brothers who are miners. A disaster at the mine almost kills one of them, and does indirectly kill the other.

JACK DREW sat on the edge of the shaft, with his foot in the loop and one hand on the rope, ready to descend. His elder brother, Tom, stood at one end of the windlass and the third man at the other. Jack paused before swinging off, looked up at his brother, and suddenly held out his hand:

'You're not going to let the sun go down, are you, Tom?'

But Tom kept both hands on the handle of the windlass and said nothing.

'Lower away!'

They lowered him to the bottom, and Tom shouldered his pick in silence and walked off to the tent. He found the tin plate and other things set ready for him on the rough table. The tea was made, the potatoes ready; he sat down at the table but could not eat. His brother's quick temper had caused the quarrel that morning; but then Jack had admitted that and apologized. Tom despised himself. He moved around anxiously and tried to smoke. He could not get Jack's last appeal out of his ears: 'You're not going to let the sun go down, are you, Tom?'

Tom found himself glancing at the sun. It was less than two

hours from sunset. He thought of the words of the old poet; the author didn't matter, but the words began to haunt him: 'Let not the sun go down upon your wrath. Let not the sun go down upon your wrath.'

The line contains good advice; for quick-tempered men are often the most sensitive, and when they let the sun go down on their wrath, that is likely to worry them in the night.

Tom started to go to the mine, but checked himself, sat down, and tried to draw comfort from a pipe. He understood his brother thoroughly, but his brother never understood him—that was where the trouble was. Presently he began thinking how Jack would worry about the quarrel and have no enthusiasm for his work. Perhaps he was worrying now, down at the end of the damp dark passage.

Tom had almost made up his mind to go below again, on some excuse, when his friend shouted from the top of the shaft:

'Tom! Tom! For God's sake come here!'

Tom's heart gave a great thump, and he ran like the wind to the shaft. All the diggers within hearing were soon on the spot. They saw at a glance what had happened. It was madness to sink a shaft without wood at the sides in that sort of ground. *The sides of the shaft were closing in!*

Tom sprang forward and shouted through the crack: 'To the face, Jack! Run to the face! To the end of the passage! Run for your life!'

Tom turned to the diggers. 'To the old workings! Bring the tools. We'll dig him out.'

A few minutes later they were at the old shaft close by and were down in the old passage. Tom knew that they were quite close to the other part of the mine. He knelt in the damp clay before the face and worked like a madman. He refused to give his place to another, and only dropped one tool to use another. He reckoned that he had six, or perhaps eight, feet to drive, and

2

he knew that the air would not last long in there, even if the roof had not already fallen and crushed his brother. Great drops of sweat stood out on Tom's forehead, and his breath came in deep sobs; but he still struck strong, savage blows into the clay before him, and the drive lengthened quickly. Once he paused a moment to listen, and then distinctly heard a sound as of a tool or stone being struck. Jack was safe!

Tom dug on until the clay suddenly fell away and left a hole about the size of a plate in the face before him.

'Thank God!' said a hoarse voice at the other side.

'All right, Jack?'

'Yes, Tom. You're just in time. I've hardly got room to stand in and I can hardly breathe.' He was crouching against the clay.

Tom fell back against the man behind him. 'Oh, God!' he cried. 'My back!'

Suddenly he struggled to his knees, and then fell forward on his hand and dragged himself close to the hole in the clay.

'Jack!' he gasped. 'Jack!'

'Right, Tom. What's the matter?'

'I've hurt my heart, Jack. Put your hand out—quick! The sun's going down.'

Jack's hand came through the hole. Tom gripped it and then fell with his face in the damp clay.

They half carried, half dragged, him from the passage; for the roof was low and they were obliged to stoop. They took him to the shaft and sent him up, fastened to the rope.

Jack soon escaped from his prison and went to the surface. He knelt on the grass by the body of his brother; the diggers gathered round and took off their hats. And the sun went down.

Ziré Buzette

MAURICE DES OMBRIAUX

Maurice des Ombriaux was born in Hainault, Belgium, in 1868.
Like many other Belgian writers, he loved the countryside; and
there he has placed the story of Ziré Buzette.

FOR many years Ziré Buzette had coughed his soul out, one of
those hard dry coughs which seem to shake and tear the chest
and make those who hear it say, 'He has not long to live.'

It was true. For a long time already Ziré Buzette had not had
long to live.

He was a plasterer during the summer, and he was seen going
out early in the morning with his bucket, brushes and sleeves,
coughing all the time.

'Poor Ziré Buzette,' said everyone. 'To do that sort of thing
with his health! It is the lime that eats away his lungs. No, he
has not long to live.'

'That miserable Ziré Buzette, how brave he is! Nothing will
persuade him to go into the hospital. He insists on working, and
all the time his blood is being poisoned. He won't last long, that's
certain.'

And Ziré went off to make the house beautiful with whitewash,
coughing on his ladder, with a face as white as his apron. He used
to whitewash kitchens and rooms too, and everyone looked after
him through sympathy. For pity, and because his prices were

On Sundays he even played the violin for young people to dance.

5

moderate, he was given work everywhere, and his services were demanded a long time ahead. Even in the humblest cottages a piece of meat was put in the oven for him.

'That poor Ziré Buzette!' they said. 'He needs strengthening. He is worn out. He won't last long.'

In the farms he was made to drink a mouthful of good wine every day. He needed it, too, not having long to live!

Yet Ziré Buzette still lived on, and on Sundays he even played the violin for young people to dance. While he played it, he coughed.

'Poor Ziré Buzette, he must be very poor if he has to get cold sitting out during a whole evening with such an illness. He has no strength in his blood. It makes your heart ache to see him shivering and coughing. Ah, no indeed, he won't last long!'

And so, at every pause, he was offered a good drink and also slices of cake. It was the least that one could do for this miserable wreck, who had not long to live. And he was liked as a musician: nobody could make people dance as he could. He played so well that even those with clumsy feet, even the beginners, went to dance and needed no persuasion. The leaders of the parties arranged with him from the beginning of the year to be quite sure that he would not fail them.

How he was spoiled! How he was 'treated'! For his sake a barrel of beer was placed on the musicians' platform. Good old Ziré Buzette must be well looked after, for he would not play much longer, and who would make them all dance then?

Ziré Buzette never refused anything, drank everything and ate everything slowly, without ever hurrying himself. To see him thus one would not have said that he had not long to live.

'It's his disease,' they thought. 'He needs food, poor fellow. Yes, one may well say so; and in spite of that he has not long to live.'

Ziré also went to the big houses of the neighbourhood to make

6

the young people dance at parties, and everywhere he was treated better than a workman or a servant. He was regarded almost as a friend. I do not know what else to say except that he had not long to live.

In winter no whitewashing was done and so, to earn his living, and to occupy his leisure hours, Ziré Buzette, still coughing, became a shoemaker. He was not, truth to tell, remarkably capable at this trade, but work never failed him. People ordered slippers from him and he made boots for children. 'Poor Ziré Buzette! He must live. It is a duty to give him work. He will not last long.'

Weak and sick, perpetually coughing, Ziré Buzette, who had not long to live, had nevertheless already buried two wives. His first had married him out of pity, it was said. 'Let us risk it,' she had thought. 'It does not bind me to much: he will not last long.'

She died of a chill.

The second had married him for his money, which was not much. 'It is a good business,' she thought. 'I have nothing, and as he will not last long I shall inherit from him. Then I can find whom I like after him.'

She died.

And now the rumour spread through the village that he was going to be married again, for the third time, to a girl who was only twenty years of age.

'Did you ever hear of such a thing?' asked the gossips. 'He has not long to live, in any case.'

'There is one who has an eye on his house and orchard,' said others. 'How shameful! She knows well enough that he won't last long.'

Ziré Buzette had his little house and piece of ground surrounded by the property of the Brothers Blairaux, the richest people in the village. One was mayor, another farmer, the third treasurer of the Charity Organization, and all three were bachelors. Big strong fellows, with powerful limbs, they looked as if they were made to live a hundred years. They owned over a hundred acres of land and bought more every year. It was said that half the village belonged to them. Their farm, field, garden and orchard made a splendid place. It was the finest property in the village. It had cost them a great deal of money and trouble. They had had to buy a bit of land from one, a ruined cottage from another, a hut here, a building there. They pulled down, filled up, levelled the ground. In order that the estate might be complete and perfect they only needed Ziré Buzette's cottage.

'He won't last long,' they said to themselves. 'We shall have it for nothing on his death.'

But their wish finally became stronger than their reason. They wanted to have the estate at once, as soon as possible; for perhaps after Ziré's death his heirs might make difficulties. Their demands might be immoderate.

After all sorts of village tricks, they started negotiations with Ziré Buzette. But their cunning plans were of no use; he would not sell. He shook his head with its pale face and said, coughing, 'Ask me anything else, sirs; but do not ask me to leave the house of my grandfathers. You know I have not long to live. Be patient. I won't go anywhere else for the short time that is left to me. I will die in the house where I was born and where all my people have died.'

He met the pressing requests of his neighbours with a gentle obstinacy. There was nothing to be done; he remained resolute. They tried in vain to frighten him with threats. They stopped dealing with him, and the mayor engaged another musician for the village festival. Ziré Buzette felt wounded by this blow, and all the villagers took his part and refused to go to the village dance. They were angry with the mayor. 'Treat a poor fellow in that way, when he has not long to live! You must be heartless!'

The Brothers Blairaux, to avoid danger, made peace with him. They increased their offers, but Ziré still refused. 'I want to die in my father's house,' he said.

8

'Sell it to us and you shall keep the use of it during your lifetime,' said the treasurer of the Charity Organization, who thought that Ziré Buzette would not last long. The idea pleased the plasterer; they discussed it and finally agreed. Ziré Buzette was to retain the use of the cottage until his death, and the Blairaux would have it then. They would also pay him rent while he lived —but only once or twice at most, for Ziré would not last long.

And the whole village said, 'Those Blairaux are fine foxes. They've bought Ziré's place cheaply; for he won't last long.'

Every year Ziré got his rent, and each time the Blairaux thought they had paid for the last time.

The mayor died without having seen the orchard joined to his land. The two other brothers paid the proper amount next time with sad faces. Then the farmer died, and Ziré, who had not long to live, continued coughing and drawing his rent. He had already received two or three times the value of his field, but the people said that this Blairaux was a lucky fellow.

A mad desire to choke the life out of the plasterer's throat made Blairaux's fingers tremble every time he had to hand over the precious gold pieces. 'Ah! There you are! Are you never going to die?' he used to say.

'Monsieur Blairaux, how can you say such things to a poor man like me, who has not long to live?' answered Ziré, coughing.

He buried the third Blairaux and then died himself, over a hundred years old. For over three-quarters of a century he had not had long to live.

Waiting for the Police

J. JEFFERSON FARJEON

Joseph Jefferson Farjeon was born in 1883, and became an actor.
However, he gave up this profession, and began to write. He has
produced about forty novels, as well as plays and short stories. In
Waiting for the Police the scene is set in Mrs. Mayton's boarding-
house, where life is nearly always very dull. But one evening, as
we shall see, it was more interesting than usual.

'I WONDER where Mr. Wainwright's gone,' said Mrs. Mayton.

It didn't matter to her in the least where he had gone. He lived
on the second floor at the back of the house, and all that mattered
about him was that he paid his three guineas a week regularly for
board and lodging, baths costing extra. But life—particularly
evening life—was terribly dull in her boarding-house, and sometimes one tried to find something interesting.

'Did he go?' asked Monty Smith.

It didn't matter to him either, but he was as polite as he was
pale.

'I thought I heard the front door close,' answered Mrs. Mayton.

'Perhaps he went out to post a letter,' suggested Miss Wicks,
without pausing in her knitting. She had knitted for seventy
years, and looked as if she would knit for another seventy.

'Or perhaps it wasn't Mr. Wainwright at all,' added Bella
Randall. She was the lovely girl of the boarding-house.

'You mean that it might have been someone else?' inquired
Mrs. Mayton.

'Yes,' agreed Bella.

They all considered the idea earnestly. Mr. Calthrop, waking suddenly, joined in the thinking without any idea of what he was thinking about.

'Perhaps it was Mr. Penbury who went out,' said Mrs. Mayton.

But it was not Mr. Penbury; for that rather unusual individual walked into the drawing-room a moment later.

His arrival interrupted the conversation, and silence returned. Penbury always had a chilling effect. He possessed a brain, and because no one understood it when he used it, it was resented. But Mrs. Mayton never allowed more than three minutes to go by without a word; and so, when the new silence had lasted three minutes, she turned to Penbury and asked, 'Was that Mr. Wainright who went out a short time ago?'

Penbury looked at her oddly. 'What makes you ask that?' he said.

'Well, I was just wondering.'

'I see,' answered Penbury slowly. The atmosphere seemed to tighten, but Miss Wicks went on knitting. 'And are you still wondering?' Penbury added.

'We decided perhaps he'd gone out to post a letter,' murmured Bella.

'No, Wainwright hasn't gone out to post a letter,' replied Penbury. 'He's dead.'

The effect was immediate and violent. Bella gave a tiny shriek. Mrs. Mayton's eyes became two startled balls of glass. Monty Smith opened his mouth and kept it open. Mr. Calthrop in a second lost all desire to sleep. Miss Wicks looked definitely interested, though she did not stop knitting. That meant nothing, however. She had promised to knit at her funeral.

'Dead?' gasped Mr. Calthrop.

'Dead,' repeated Penbury. 'He is lying on the floor of his room. He is not a pleasant sight.'

11

Monty leapt up and then sat down again.

'You—you don't mean—?' he gulped.

'That is exactly what I mean,' replied Penbury.

There had been countless silences in Mrs. Mayton's drawing-room, but never a silence like this one. Miss Wicks broke it.

'Shouldn't the police be sent for?' she suggested.

'The police have already been sent for,' said Penbury. 'I 'phoned the police station just before coming into the room.'

'God bless my soul!' said Mr. Calthrop.

'How long—that is—when do you expect—?' stammered Monty.

'The police? I should say in two or three minutes,' replied Penbury. His voice suddenly lost its mocking tone and became practical. 'Shall we try to make use of these two or three minutes? We shall all be questioned, and perhaps we can be sure of the facts before they arrive.'

'But this is nothing to do with any of us, sir!' exclaimed Mr. Calthrop.

'The police will not necessarily believe that,' answered Penbury. 'That is why I suggest that we should consider where we all were at the time. I am not a doctor, but I estimate from my brief examination of the body that it has not been dead for more than an hour. It cannot, of course, be more than an hour and a half, since it is now ten past nine and at twenty to eight we saw him leave the dining-room for his bedroom—'

'How do you know he went to his bedroom?' interrupted Miss Wicks.

'Because I had a headache and followed him upstairs to go to my room to get some aspirin; and my room is opposite his. Now, if I am right, he was killed between ten minutes past eight and ten minutes past nine. Therefore anyone who can prove that he or she remained in this room all that time need not worry.'

He looked round inquiringly.

'We've all been out of the room,' Miss Wicks announced.

'That is unfortunate,' murmured Penbury.

'But so have *you*,' exclaimed Monty nervously.

'Yes—so I have,' replied Penbury. 'Then I will speak first. At twenty to eight I followed Wainwright up to the second floor. Before going into his room he made an odd remark which is worth repeating. "There's somebody in this house who doesn't like me very much," he said. "Only one?" I answered. "You're luckier than I am." Then he went into his room, and that was the last time I saw him alive. I went to my room. I took two aspirins. I went into the bathroom to wash them down with a drink of water. My water-bottle needs filling again, Mrs. Mayton. Then, as my head was still bad, I thought a walk would be a good idea, and I went out. I kept out till approximately nine o'clock, and then I came back. The door that you heard closing, Mrs. Mayton, was not Wainwright going out. It was myself coming in.'

'Wait a moment!' cried Bella. 'How did you know Mrs. Mayton heard the front door close? You weren't here!'

Penbury regarded her with interest and respect. 'Intelligent,' he murmured.

'Don't take too long thinking of an answer!' glared Mr. Calthrop.

'I don't need any time at all to think of an answer,' replied Penbury sharply. 'I know because I listened outside the door. But may I finish my statement in my own way? Thank you! When I came back I went up to my room, and on the floor I found a handkerchief. It wasn't mine. It hadn't been there when I left. I wondered whether it was Wainwright's. I went into his room to ask if the handkerchief was his. I found him lying on the floor near his bed. Dressed, of course. On his back. Head towards the window, one arm stretched towards the fireplace. Stabbed through the heart. No weapon there, but it looks a small wound, but deep. The window was fastened. Whoever did it entered

13

through the door. I left the room and locked the door. I came down and telephoned and on the way I stopped outside this door and heard what you all said.'

'Why did you sit here for three minutes without telling us?' demanded Mrs. Mayton hotly.

'I was watching you,' answered Penbury coolly.

'Well, I call that a poor explanation,' exclaimed Mr. Calthrop. 'Who can prove you were out all that time?'

'At half past eight I had a cup of coffee in Junkers Street. That's over a mile away. It's not proof, I admit, but they know me there, and it may help. Well, who's next?'

'I am,' said Bella. 'I left the room to blow my nose. I went to my room for a handkerchief. And here it *is*!' she concluded, producing it triumphantly.

'How long were you out of the room?' said Penbury.

'Five minutes, I should say.'

'A long time to get a handkerchief! What about you, Mr. Calthrop? We all know you walk in your sleep. A week ago you walked into my room, didn't you? Have *you* lost a handkerchief?'

Mr. Calthrop glared. 'What the devil do you mean?' he exclaimed.

'Has Mr. Calthrop slept during the past hour?' asked Penbury.

'What rubbish!' he cried. 'Did I leave this room without knowing it and kill Wainwright for—for no reason at all?' He swallowed and calmed down. 'I left the room, sir, about twenty minutes ago to fetch the evening paper, and here it is!'

Penbury shrugged his shoulders. 'I should be the last to reject such a loud statement,' he said, 'but let me suggest that you tell the police with less emphasis. Mr. Smith?'

Monty Smith had followed the conversation anxiously, and he had his story ready. Speaking slowly and carefully he answered, 'This is why I left the room. Mr. Wainwright lent me his key this afternoon, when I lost mine, and I went out to return it.

But on the first floor I met Mrs. Mayton, who asked me to help her with the curtain of the landing window. It had come off some of its hooks. I did so and then returned to the drawing-room with her. You'll remember, all of you, that we returned together.'

'That's right,' nodded Mrs. Mayton. 'And the reason *I* went out was to fix the curtain.'

Penbury looked at Monty hard. 'Where's the key?' he asked.

'What? Oh, of course! The curtain put it out of my mind. It's still in my pocket.'

'And you didn't go up to his room?'

'No! Thank goodness!'

Penbury shrugged his shoulders again. He did not seem satisfied. But he turned now to Miss Wicks, and the old lady inquired, while her needles moved busily, 'My turn?'

'If you'll be so good,' answered Penbury.

'I understand. There's no need to apologize. Well, I left the drawing-room to fetch some knitting needles. The steel ones that I'm using now. My room, as you know, is on the second floor, and after I'd got the needles I was just about to come down when I heard Mr. Wainwright's cough—'

'What! You heard him cough?' interrupted Penbury. 'What time was that?'

'Just before nine, I think it was,' said Miss Wicks. 'Oh, that irritating cough! How it gets on one's nerves. Morning, noon and night. Enough to send one mad.' She paused, and the tense atmosphere grew tenser. 'Your door was open, Mr. Penbury, and I went in to ask if we could do something about that cough. But you were out. You've just told us where. And suddenly, when I heard Mr. Wainwright coughing again across the passage —well, I felt that I couldn't bear it any more. I knocked at his door—it was my handkerchief that you found in your room, Mr. Penbury. I must have dropped it there.'

She paused again, and Penbury murmured, 'Go on.'

She turned on him fiercely. Mr. Calthrop nearly jumped out of his chair. Monty felt sweat dripping down his neck. Bella twisted her fingers together to prevent herself from shrieking. Mrs. Mayton sat rigid.

'Will you stop interrupting?' shouted the old woman.

Penbury moistened his lips. For a few moments Miss Wicks knitted rapidly, the steel points of the needles making the only sound in the room. Then she continued in a queer, hard voice.

' "Come in!" called Mr. Wainwright. "I'm coming in," I called back. And I went in. And there he stood smiling at me. "You haven't come to complain of my cough again, have you?" he asked. "No," I answered. "I've come to cure it." And I plunged a steel knitting-needle into his heart—like this!'

She stretched out a bony hand, and with amazing strength stabbed a cushion.

The next instant there came a knocking on the front door. 'The police!' gasped Mr. Calthrop. But no one moved. They listened tensely. Then they heard someone open the front door; they heard footsteps entering.

A moment later they heard Mr. Wainwright's dry cough.

'Yes! And I heard it when he went out ten minutes ago,' smiled Miss Wicks. 'But thank you very much indeed, Mr. Penbury. It was all very interesting, and before you came in I was as bored as the others.'

One or the Other

RUPERT CROFT-COOKE

Rupert Croft-Cooke was educated at Tonbridge School, and lives in Tangier. He has published about sixty books, including poems. Some of his short stories appeared for the first time in newspapers and other periodicals, and were later collected and published in book form. *One or the Other* is in the collection entitled *A Football for the Brigadier* (1950). In this story Mrs. Shaw talks to a young man about her choice of a husband: and as her house is pleasant and comfortable, it is evident that she has chosen well.

'How pleasant it is to have money!' Mrs. Shaw might have been thinking as she sat behind the tray and tilted her old and beautiful silver teapot. Everything about her and about her home suggested excellent taste helped by endless money at the bank. And although it would be unfair to call her vulgar she was not afraid to show a frank pleasure in her great possessions.

'I am so glad you like the picture,' she said to the artistic young man who was carefully balanced in the chair before her. 'My husband bought it for me last week. I've always wanted a Brueghel.'

'Exquisite,' stated the young man. 'You're very lucky.'

Mrs. Shaw smiled, her delicate eyebrows rising prettily. Her hands were still, as if they had been modelled in pink wax to exhibit her beautiful rings. She had not that irritating restlessness which is so common. She did not touch her hair or smooth her dress, she did not play with a little dog or with the teacups. She knew the value of repose.

'I am so glad you like the picture.'

18

'Lucky?' she said. 'I don't believe in luck. It is all a matter of choice.'

If the young man thought this a curious word to apply to the possession of wealth, he did not say so. He nodded with just sufficient encouragement, and Mrs. Shaw continued.

'Well, it was in my case.'

'You just chose to be rich?' said the young man, not wholly concealing his envy.

'You may describe it like that. Fifteen years ago I was an awkward schoolgirl . . .'

She paused to give him time to disagree, but he was busy counting the years. He decided, but silently, that she must have stayed very late at school.

'*You* understand,' Mrs. Shaw continued; 'always thinking of games and such things, and with that terrible quality called, I believe, a healthy natural charm. I cannot quite understand it now, but there were two young men in love with me.'

Her listener seemed determined not to say the right things when she gave him the opportunity. He showed no impatience, though he *was* wondering how he would turn the conversation to more profitable subjects. But he was too bad-tempered to say any of the things that were expected of him.

'One of them was a penniless young art-student,' said Mrs. Shaw. 'A romantic, lovable youth who could never save any money. He had no idea of business, and no hope of ever receiving any money from his relations, but he loved me and I suppose I loved him too. The other was the son of a successful business man with a keen sense of the value of things. He could expect a successful and prosperous life. In a strong and healthy sort of way he might have been called good-looking. And I'm afraid he loved me as much as the art-student.'

The young man in the arm-chair saved himself from yawning by speech.

'Quite a difficult choice,' he said.

'It was. On the one hand romantic love in a poor street, with dirty tea-things all over the place and rather unwashed visitors; but real love. On the other hand, a charming home, an easy life, nice friends, travel, clothes, all the things one wanted. If *things* are what one ever wants.'

Mrs. Shaw's voice had grown a little sad.

'I lived for a year in an agony of indecision. No other possibility made its appearance, and it was perfectly clear that I should have to choose one or the other. Yet whichever it was, there would inevitably be regrets. At last . . .' Mrs. Shaw's glance wandered round her lovely room, which had provided a magazine called *Tasteful Homes* with a large number of photographs. 'At last I decided.'

It was at this rather dramatic point that the conversation was interrupted by the entrance of a handsome, grey-haired man who was an excellent advertisement for his tailor, and who fitted his background like a figure set in a fine picture. He kissed Mrs. Shaw, who introduced the young man to her husband.

There followed fifteen minutes of good, natural conversation, during which Mr. Shaw mentioned that he had met 'poor old Dick Rogers' today and had lent him some money.

'Nice of you, dear,' said Mrs. Shaw without interest.

Presently Mr. Shaw went out.

'Poor old Dick Rogers,' sighed Mrs. Shaw. 'I expect you have guessed. That was the other man. My husband has never been difficult about him.'

'Good,' said her listener briefly, and because he could not think of a more intelligent reply. His own time was coming.

'I don't know how my husband has time to look after everyone. He's so terribly busy. His portrait of the Admiral . . .'

'Portrait?' gasped the young man, suddenly sitting up straight in his chair.

'Yes, portrait,' said Mrs. Shaw. 'Oh, didn't I make that clear? It was the artist I married, of course. And now I think it's time for a drink. How do you feel?'

The young man nodded, but seemed quite unable to make his feelings known.

The Cobbler Blondeau

BONAVENTURE DES PERIERS

Bonaventure des Periers was born of a noble family in Burgundy about the year 1500, and became an author. In 1536 he entered the service of Marguerite, Queen of Navarre, whose secretary he became. One of his books, which appeared in 1537, made him many enemies, and he left Paris and settled at Lyons. There, in 1544, he put an end to his life by falling upon his sword.

He was a man of much worldly wisdom, and in some ways resembled Voltaire. The story given here is well known in France, and shows something of the writer's philosophy of life.

THERE was a cobbler of Paris who was called Blondeau. He lived near the Croix du Tiroir, and there he mended shoes, taking life joyfully and loving good wine above everything. And he was ready to share it with all who came. All day long he sang and delighted his neighbours. He was never mournful except on two occasions in his life.

The first of these was when he found an iron pot in an old wall. It contained a large quantity of antique pieces of money, some of silver and some of gold. He did not know what they were worth, and he lost his cheerfulness. His songs ceased, and he thought only of his iron pot.

'If the money is not in use now,' he thought to himself, 'I shall not be able to buy bread or wine with it. If I take it to the gold-smiths, they will either trick me, and I shall lose the treasure, or they will demand a large share of the find and I shall not get half of what it is worth.'

Then he grew afraid that he had not hidden the pot properly, and that someone would steal it from him. He was continually leaving his shelter to go and see if it was safe. He was in great trouble, but at last he came to his senses.

'What!' he said. 'I do nothing but think of my pot! Everyone who knows my habits must see that something has happened to me. The thing only brings me bad luck!'

So he took up the treasure gaily, and threw it into the Seine. Thus he drowned his sadness.

On another occasion he was much upset by a gentleman who dwelt opposite his shelter. This gentleman had a monkey that played a thousand tricks on poor Blondeau. For the animal watched him from a high window when he was cutting his leather, and noticed how he did it. And as soon as Blondeau went to dinner or left on some other business, the monkey came down and ran into Blondeau's shelter, took his knife and cut the leather in imitation of the cobbler. And this happened every time that Blondeau went away.

The poor man at last dared not go out to eat or drink or leave his business without locking up all his leather. And if sometimes he forgot to shut it away, the monkey never forgot to cut it to bits. The thing angered him greatly, but he was unable to hurt the monkey for fear of his master. Yet he became very annoyed and resolved to find a means of avenging himself.

The monkey imitated everything that he saw the cobbler do. If Blondeau sharpened his knife, the monkey sharpened it after him. If he put a boot between his knees, the monkey came and took a boot and put it between his knees. Blondeau noticed all this.

Having studied the matter in this way, he sharpened his knife until it cut like a razor. Then, when the monkey came out to watch him, he took up the knife and drew it backwards and forwards over his throat. And when he had done this long enough to attract the notice of the monkey, he left his shelter and went out to dinner.

The monkey came down in great haste; for it wished to try this new game that it had just been studying. It took the knife and put it against its throat, drawing it backwards and forwards as Blondeau had done. The animal, however, brought the knife too close, and cut its throat so badly that it died within an hour.

The Accursed House

EMILE GABORIAU

Emile Gaboriau (1835–73) published various writings before he found his true gift in *L'Affaire Lerouge* (1866), one of the earliest detective stories. A long list of other stories of this kind followed, and the writer has remained famous ever since. Yet *The Accursed House* proves that he could write a good short story when he wished. The title must not be allowed to darken the reader's thoughts: for it is a joke. The owners of property in towns and cities usually raise their rents when they can; this tale shows what happened when a good-natured owner of property in Paris did the opposite.

THE Viscount of B—, a pleasant and charming young man, was peacefully enjoying an income of 30,000 livres yearly when, unfortunately for him, his uncle died. This uncle, a man who had always hated spending money, left all his wealth, amounting to nearly two millions, to the young viscount.

When examining his uncle's business papers, the young man found that he was now the owner of a house in the Rue de la Victoire. This building brought in, clear of taxes, rents amounting to 82,000 francs a year.

'Too much; too much, entirely,' thought the generous viscount. 'My uncle was too hard; the rents are too high. When one bears a great name like mine, one should not act like a thief. I will begin tomorrow to lower my rents, and my tenants will bless me.'

With this excellent purpose in his mind, the viscount sent

immediately for the *concierge* of the building, who came promptly and bowed low before the nobleman.

'Bernard, my friend,' said the viscount, 'go at once and notify all your tenants that I lower their rents by one-third.'

The unheard-of word 'lower' fell like a brick on Bernard's head. But he quickly recovered himself; he had heard badly; he had not understood.

'*Lower* the rents?' he stammered. 'Monsieur is joking. Lower! Monsieur, of course, means raise the rents.'

'I was never more serious in my life, my friend,' the viscount replied; 'I said, and I repeat it, lower the rents.'

This time the *concierge* was surprised to the point of bewilderment. He was so upset that he lost all restraint.

'Monsieur has not thought about this,' he said. 'Monsieur will regret this evening. Lower the tenants' rents! Never was such a thing known, Monsieur! If the lodgers should learn of it, what would they think of Monsieur? What would people say in the neighbourhood? Truly—'

'Monsieur Bernard, my friend,' interrupted the viscount, 'I prefer to be obeyed at once when I give an order. You hear me. Go!'

Staggering like a drunken man, Monsieur Bernard left the house. All his ideas were upset. Was he, or was he not, the plaything of a bad dream? Was he himself Pierre Bernard, or Bernard somebody else?

'Lower his rents; lower his rents!' he repeated. 'It is not to be believed. If the lodgers had complained . . . but they have not complained. On the contrary, they are all good payers. Ah! if his uncle knew of this, he would rise from his tomb! The nephew has gone mad, that's certain. Lower the rents! This young man should appear before a family council. He will come to a bad end. Who knows what he will do next? Perhaps his lunch this morning was too good.'

Bernard was so pale with emotion when he reached his lodge that his wife and daughter Amanda exclaimed together:

'Good heavens! What is it? What has happened to you now?'

'Nothing,' he replied in a changed voice. 'Absolutely nothing.'

'You are deceiving me,' said Madame Bernard. 'You are concealing something from me. Do not spare me. Speak! I am strong. What did the new master tell you? Does he want to get rid of us?'

'I wish it were only that! But just think: he told me with his own lips, he told me—ah! you will never believe me—'

'Yes, yes. Please go on. Please.'

'You will have it then! Well, then, he told me, he ordered me to notify all the tenants that—*he lowered their rents by one-third!* Did you hear what I said? *Lowered* the rents of the tenants—'

But neither Madame nor Mademoiselle Bernard heard him to the end. They were twisting with violent laughter.

'Lower!' they repeated. 'Ah, what a good joke! What a strange man you are! Lower the tenants' rents!'

But Bernard lost his temper and insisted that they must treat him seriously in his own lodge. Then his wife lost her temper too, and a quarrel followed. Madame Bernard declared that Monsieur Bernard, beyond doubt, had received this fantastic order from the bottom of a glass of wine in the restaurant at the corner.

The couple would undoubtedly have come to blows if Mademoiselle Amanda had not prevented a fight. And finally Madame Bernard, who did not wish to be thought insane, ran to the viscount's house to find out the facts. Bernard had spoken truly. With her own two ears, ornamented with big rings, she heard the incredible word. But, as she was a wise woman, she demanded 'a bit of writing' to relieve herself of all responsibility.

All that evening in the lodge father, mother and daughter argued. Should they obey? Or should they warn the relatives of this mad young man? They decided to obey.

Next morning, Bernard, buttoning himself in his best coat, went to announce his great news to all the tenants.

Ten minutes later the building in the Rue de la Victoire was in a state of disturbance impossible to describe. People who for forty years had lived on the same floor, and never honoured each other even by a touch of the hat, now gathered together and chatted eagerly.

'Do you know, Monsieur?'

'It is very extraordinary.'

'It is unheard-of!'

'The owner has lowered my rent!'

'One-third, is it not? Mine also!'

'Astounding! It *must* be a mistake.'

In spite of what the Bernard family said, and in spite of the 'bit of writing', there were many who doubted. Three of them actually wrote to the viscount to tell him what had happened and to warn him that the *concierge* had lost his mind. But the viscount replied, confirming what Bernard had said. After that, doubt was impossible, and comment began.

'*Why* has the owner lowered the rents?'

'Yes, *why*?'

'He must certainly have grave reasons for a step like this. An intelligent man, a man of good sense, would never deprive himself of good money just for the simple pleasure of depriving himself. There must be a reason. There must be powerful or terrible circumstances.'

And each said to himself, '*There is something behind all this.*'

'But what?'

They tried to imagine what it was. From the top to the bottom of the building they sought the answer in the depths of their brains. Every lodger had the thoughtful appearance of a man who is trying with all his strength to solve an impossible problem, and everywhere there was a vague disquiet, as happens when one

28

finds oneself in the presence of an unpleasant mystery. Someone even suggested that this man must have committed a great and unknown crime, and was now trying to pay back his debt to society.

'It is not a pleasant idea,' they thought, 'to be living thus side by side with a rascal. No! Not at all! Even if he is sorry for what he has done, he might do something else of the same sort!'

'The house, perhaps, was badly built,' another suggested.

Everyone knew one thing: it was certainly very old!

True! And it had been necessary to prop it up when they dug the drain last year in the month of March.

'Perhaps the roof is bad,' suggested a tenant on the fifth floor.

'Or perhaps,' said a lodger right at the top, 'there is a machine for making false money in the basement. I have often heard strange sounds at night.'

The opinion of another was that the house was full of spies, and the gentleman on the first floor believed that the owner intended to set fire to the house so as to obtain great sums of money from the insurance companies.

Then very strange things (as they all declared) began to happen. On the sixth and top floors unusual noises were heard for which there was no explanation whatever. Then, one night, the nurse of an old lady on the fourth floor went to steal some wine from the cellar and met the ghost of the dead owner with a receipt for rent in one hand.

From anxiety their feelings turned to fright and from fright to terror. The gentleman of the first floor, who had valuables in his rooms, made up his mind to go, and sent in notice by his clerk.

Bernard went to tell the owner, who replied, 'All right; let the fool go!'

But the next day a man on the second floor, though he had nothing to fear for his valuables, imitated the gentleman beneath him. Others on the fifth floor followed his example.

From that moment it was a general collapse. By the end of the week everybody had given notice. Everyone awaited some frightful disaster. They slept no more. They watched all night in groups. The frightened servants declared that they would leave the accursed house, and remained only when their wages were multiplied by three.

Bernard himself was no more than a ghost. The fever of fear had made him a mere shadow. Meanwhile twenty-three notices swung at the front of the house. Each of them said, 'To let.' Sometimes Bernard took visitors to see the different lodgings. 'You can have your choice,' he said. 'All the tenants have given notice. They do not know exactly why, but things have happened. Oh, yes, *things!* A mystery, never known before: *the owner has lowered his rents!'*

And the visitors fled, terrified.

Twenty-three tenants and their furniture left. From top to bottom the building was empty. The rats themselves, finding nothing to live on, left it too. Only the *concierge* remained, grey-green with fear, in his lodge, troubled by frightful dreams and miserable noises that made his hair stand on end. Madame Bernard slept no better than he did. And Amanda, in order to get away from her father's home, married a young hairdresser whom she had never before been able to endure.

At last, one morning, after a more frightful dream than usual, Bernard himself took the great decision, went to the viscount, gave up his keys and escaped.

And now in the Rue de la Victoire the accursed house stands empty. Dust lies thick on it, grass grows in the court. No tenant ever goes there now. And the reputation of the building is so bad that even neighbouring houses on each side of it have also gone down in value. Lower one's rents! Who would think of such a thing?

Captain Obstinate

ANONYMOUS

This story, whose author has remained unknown, was first published in 1854. It is a tale of Napoleon's retreat from Moscow (1812) told by an old soldier who has lost an arm in the wars.

ONE fine evening in the month of July, an old soldier of Napoleon's grand army, who had left one of his arms on the field of battle, was seated at the door of his pretty cottage.

He was surrounded by a group of young villagers, who were noisily reminding him of his promise to tell them some of his military adventures.

After a moment of pretended resistance to their wishes, the old man took his pipe from his mouth and thus began his tale:

'My story begins, my friends, on 6th November, 1812, a short time after the battle of Wiazma. We retreated, not from the Russians, for they were at a respectful distance from our camp, but from the sharp and bitter cold of their horrible country, a cold more terrible to us than the Russians, Austrians, and Bavarians all put together.

'During the preceding days our officers had told us that we were approaching Smolensko, where we should get food, fire, brandy, and shoes; but in the meantime we were perishing in the ice, and continually attacked by the Cossacks.

'We had marched for six hours without stopping to take breath; for we knew that to rest was certain death. An icy wind blew the snow in our faces and from time to time we stumbled

31

over the frozen corpse of a comrade. We neither spoke nor sang; even complaints were no longer heard, and that was a bad sign.

'I marched by the side of my captain. He was short, strongly built, rough and severe, but brave and true as the blade of his sword. We called him "Captain Obstinate"; for when once he said a thing, it was fixed. He never changed his opinions. He had been wounded at Wiazma, and his usually red face was terribly pale. A torn white handkerchief, stained with blood, was bound round his head and made him look even paler.

'All at once I saw him stagger on his legs like a drunken man, and then fall like a block to the ground.

' "Captain!" I said, bending over him, "you cannot remain here."

' "You see that I can, since I do it," replied he.

' "Captain," said I, "you must not give way." I lifted him up in my arms and tried to put him on his feet. He leaned on me and attempted to walk, but it was in vain. He fell again, dragging me down with him.

' "Jobin," he said, "all is over. Leave me here and rejoin your company as quickly as possible. One word before you go: at Voreppe, near Grenoble, lives a good woman, eighty-two years of age, my mother. Go and see her; embrace her for me, and tell her that—that—tell her what you wish, but give her this purse and my cross. It is all I have! Now go."

' "Is that all, Captain?"

' "That is all. God bless you! Make haste. Farewell!" My friends, I do not know how it happened, but I felt two tears roll down my cheeks.

' "No, Captain," I cried. "I will not leave you. Either you come with me, or I will remain with you."

' "I forbid you to remain."

' "You may put me under arrest, then, if you like, but at present you must let me do as I please."

32

'Captain!' I said, bending over him.

' "You are an insolent fellow."

' "Very good, Captain, but you must come with me."

'He bit his lips with rage, but said no more.

'I lifted him and carried him on my shoulders like a sack. You can easily imagine that with such a burden I could not keep pace with my comrades. In fact, I soon lost sight of them, and could see nothing around me but the white and silent plain. I still walked on but presently I saw some Cossacks galloping towards me at a furious speed.

'The captain was by this time completely unconscious and I resolved never to abandon him, whatever it cost me. I laid him down on the ground and covered him with snow. Then I crept beneath a heap of dead bodies, but left my eyes at liberty.

'Presently the Cossacks came up and began to strike with their lances right and left as we lay beneath the horses' feet. One of these heavy beasts set its foot upon my right arm, and crushed it.

'My friends, I did not speak or stir. I put my right hand into my mouth to stop the cry of torture which nearly escaped from me, and in a few minutes the Cossacks had gone.

'When the last of them had disappeared, I quitted my refuge and uncovered the captain. To my joy he gave some signs of life. I was able to carry him with my one arm towards a rock which offered a sort of shelter, and then I laid myself by his side, wrapping my cloak round us both.

'The night had closed in and the snow continued to fall. The last of our comrades had long since disappeared, and the only sound that broke the stillness of the night was the whistle of a bullet, or the howling of the wolves eating the corpses that lay stretched on the snow. God knows what thoughts passed through my soul during that dreadful night, which, I felt sure, would be my last upon earth. But I remembered the prayer that my mother had taught me long before when I was a child, and I earnestly repeated it now.

'My children, that helped me a good deal. Remember that a sincere prayer is sure to comfort you. I felt astonishingly calm in my place by the captain. But the time passed, and I became partly unconscious. Then I saw a group of French officers approaching. Before I had time to speak to them, their chief, a little man, stepped forward towards me and said:

' "What are you doing here? Why are you away from your comrades?"

' "For two good reasons," said I, pointing first to the captain, and then to my bleeding arm.

' "The man is speaking the truth, sire," said one of those who followed him. "I saw him marching behind the others and carrying this officer on his back."

'The Emperor—for, my friends, it was he—gave me one of those glances that only he could give, and said, "It is well. You have done very well." Then, opening his cloak, he took the cross which decorated his green coat and gave it to me. At that instant I was no longer hungry, no longer cold; I felt no more pain in my arm than if that awkward beast had never touched it.

' "Davoust," added the Emperor, addressing the officer who had spoken to him, "see this man and his captain placed in one of the baggage-waggons. Farewell!" And making a motion of the hand towards me, he went away.'

Here the old soldier stopped, and began to smoke his pipe again.

'But tell us what happened to Captain Obstinate,' cried many impatient voices.

'The captain recovered, and is now a general on the retired list. But the best joke was that, as soon as he got well, he put me under arrest for fifteen days as a punishment for my dis-obedience.

'This circumstance came to the ears of Napoleon, and after laughing heartily he not only caused me to be set free, but promoted me to the rank of sergeant. As to the honour he gave me, my children, here is the ribbon at my button-hole; but the cross I wear next to my heart.'

And opening his vest, he showed his eager audience the precious cross, suspended from his neck in a little bag.

At the Palace of Justice

ALPHONSE DAUDET

Alphonse Daudet (1840–97) was born at Nîmes, and had an unhappy boyhood. He tried teaching, but left that to write poems
and to become a journalist. He became famous for his short
stories and novels, and was accused of imitating Dickens.

He has a charming style of his own; and the material of his
writing came from his own experiences and surroundings. One of
his books is a bitter attack on the French Academy, to which he
never belonged. Towards the end of his life he suffered from
sleeplessness and ill health.

The short story given here is a love story, but one of an unusual
kind.

I DO not know why, but I can never enter the Palace of Justice
without a feeling of uneasiness. Those great courts, that vast stone
staircase, the great age of the building, the height of the windows,
the damp on the walls—all these give you a taste of the neighbouring prison. There are the noises too: the sounds of weeping
and of carriages that pass, shaking the arches: these are like the
breath of a factory, the machine of justice at work. Hearing them,
one wants to make oneself small, for fear of being caught.

I was there one morning for the purpose of trying to help a
poor fellow in trouble, and there, in the middle of these shadows,
I saw two creatures in love. At the end of a bench was seated a
young girl, as quiet as a working woman who is waiting for the
price of her day's labour. The girl wore the sad clothes of a
prisoner with an air of repose and well-being, as though prison

37

were the best thing she had found in all her life. The guard who sat beside her seemed to find her much to his taste, and they laughed together softly. At the other end of the room, in the shadow, was seated the man who loved this girl. She had not seen him at first; but as soon as her eyes became accustomed to the darkness, she noticed him and trembled. 'Why, that's Pignou! Hey, Pignou!'

The guard silenced her. Prisoners are forbidden to talk to each other.

'Oh, I beg you! Only one word!' she said, leaning far towards the distant part of the room.

But the guard would not agree. 'No—no—it can't be done—only if you have some message to give him, tell it to me and I will repeat it to him.'

Then a conversation was started between this girl and her Pignou, with the guard as interpreter.

With great emotion, without heeding the people around her, she began, 'Tell him I have never loved anyone except him; that I will never love another in all my life.'

The guard made a number of steps forwards and became more serious. Then he repeated, 'She says she has never loved anyone but you and that she'll never love another.'

I heard a grumbling, a confused stammering that must have been Pignou's answer. Then the guard went back with slow steps towards the bench.

'What did he say?' demanded the girl anxiously, and as if she had waited too long. 'Well, tell me what he said.'

'He said he was very miserable.'

Then her emotion and the custom of the noisy city made her cry out loud, 'Don't be weary, my friend. The good days will come again!' In her voice, though still young, there was something of pity, almost like a mother's voice. Plainly this was a woman of the people, with courage in trouble.

From the far end of the room a voice replied, the voice of Pignou, a voice of wine and alcohol: 'The good old days! I'll have them at the end of my five years.'

The guard cried, 'Hush! Keep quiet!' But too late.

A door had opened, and the examining magistrate himself appeared. His mouth was thin and evil, the eye distrustful; he was one of those men who think they have a criminal before them always, like the doctors of the insane who see madmen everywhere. That one, in particular, had a certain way of looking at you, so annoying and so insulting that you felt guilty without having done anything. With one glance from his eye he terrified everyone. 'What does all this noise mean? Try to do your duty a little better,' he said to the guard. Then he closed his door sharply.

The guard, rebuked in public, ashamed, red in the face, looked around for someone upon whom to lay the blame. But the little girl said nothing more and Pignou sat quietly on his bench. All at once he perceived me, and as I was at the door of the hall, he took me by the arm and jerked me round brutally.

'What are you doing there, you?'

The Piece of String

GUY DE MAUPASSANT

Guy de Maupassant (1850–93), who came of a noble Norman family, was born with madness in him and was mad when he died. He often (and usually with injustice) attacked his own countrymen; but as a writer of short stories he has rarely been equalled for originality and forceful effect.

The Piece of String, one of his best-known stories, is a fierce study of Norman life, in which the underlying bitterness is somewhat hidden by the interest of the story.

ON all the roads round Goderville the peasants and their wives were making their way towards the little town, for it was market day. The men were walking heavily, their bodies thrust forward with every movement of their long legs. They were misshapen from their heavy work and all the back-breaking tasks that make up the life of the agricultural labourer.

Sometimes one of them was leading a cow on a long rope, while the wife urged the animal on from behind with branches still covered with leaves. The women were carrying on their arms large baskets, from which the heads of chickens or ducks stuck out. They walked with a shorter, more active step than the men, and their thin figures were wrapped in little shawls.

On the square at Goderville there was a confused mass of animals and human beings. The sharp voices made an unceasing noise, and from time to time there rose a great roar of laughter from some cheerful soul. Everywhere there was the smell of cowhouses and milk—the powerful smell of men and animals which is characteristic of those who work on the land.

Master Hauchecorne, of Bréauté, had just reached Goderville and was making his way towards the market square, when he caught sight of a small piece of string on the ground. Master Hauchecorne, like all true Normans, liked to save money when he could, and decided that it was always worth while picking up anything that might be useful. So he bent down with some difficulty, for he suffered from rheumatism. He picked up the bit of thin string from the ground and was preparing to roll it up carefully when he caught sight of Master Malandain, the saddler, at his shop-door watching him. They had had a difference of opinion in the past about some small matter, and had been un-friendly ever since because neither was ready to forgive.

Master Hauchecorne felt somehow ashamed at being seen by his enemy like this, looking for a bit of string in the dirt. He quickly hid his treasure under his clothes, and slipped it into a trouser pocket. Then he pretended to look for something that he could not find, and soon went on towards the square, leaning forward, bent double by his rheumatism.

He was immediately lost in the noisy crowd, where everyone was bargaining keenly. The peasants were examining the cows; they went away and came back again, hesitating, always afraid of being tricked, unable to make up their minds. They watched the seller's expression, trying to understand his cunning or find the defects of the animal.

The women had taken out the chickens, which now lay on the ground, tied by the legs, with terror in their eyes. They listened to the bids, refused to lower their prices, hard-faced and cool; or they suddenly made up their minds to accept the lower price which was offered, and shouted after the buyer, who was slowly walking away, 'Right you are, Master Anthime; you can have it.'

Then gradually the crowd grew thinner, and those who lived

too far away to go home went to the inns. All the aristocracy of the plough took its meals at Master Jourdain's, innkeeper and horse-dealer, a cunning fellow who had made his money. Dishes were brought in, and carried out empty. Everybody was talking about the business done, what each had bought and sold. Questions were asked about the harvest. The weather was good for the green crops, but rather damp for the wheat.

Suddenly the roll of a drum was heard in the courtyard in front of the inn. All the diners got up at once, except a few who were not interested, and ran to the door or windows with their mouths still full.

When he had finished his roll on the drum, the town-crier read out his notice with pauses in the wrong places, so that it made nonsense:

'Notice is given to the inhabitants of Goderville and in general to all those present at the market that there has been lost this morning on the Beuzeville road between nine and ten o'clock a black leather wallet containing five hundred francs and some business papers. Anyone finding the wallet is requested to bring it without delay to the Town Hall or to Master Fortuné Houlbrèque, of Manneville. A reward of twenty francs is offered.'

Then the man went away. The deep notes of the drum and the town-crier's announcement were repeated a second time in the distance.

Everyone began discussing the loss, wondering whether Master Houlbrèque had any chance of recovering the wallet or not.

At last the meal came to an end. They were finishing their coffee when the police sergeant appeared at the door and asked:

'Is Master Hauchecorne here?'

Master Hauchecorne, who was sitting at the far end of the table, replied, 'Yes, I'm here.'

The sergeant went on, 'Master Hauchecorne, will you be so good as to come with me to the Town Hall? The Mayor would like to speak to you.'

The peasant, surprised and worried, hurriedly swallowed his drink and got up. He was even more bent than in the morning, for the first few steps after a rest were particularly painful. He followed the sergeant, repeating, 'I'm here, I'm here.'

The Mayor was waiting for him, sitting in an armchair. He was the local lawyer—a fat, important man, fond of important language.

'Master Hauchecorne,' he said, 'you were seen this morning to pick up the wallet lost by Master Houlbrèque, of Manneville, on the Beuzeville road.'

The peasant, astonished, looked at the Mayor; he was already frightened at the suspicion that had fallen upon him, without quite knowing why.

'Me? I picked up the wallet, did I?'

'Yes, you.'

'On my honour I know nothing about it.'

'You were seen.'

'Who saw me?'

'Master Malandain, the saddler.'

Then the old man remembered, understood, and red with anger cried, 'So he saw me, did he, the devil? This is what he saw me pick up, this piece of string. Look, sir!'

And feeling in the depths of his pocket, he pulled out the little bit of string.

But the Mayor shook his head in disbelief. 'You'll never persuade me,' he said, 'that Master Malandain, who is a reliable man, mistook a piece of string for a wallet.'

The peasant was now in a furious temper. 'But it's God's truth. It's the whole truth and nothing but the truth.'

The Mayor went on, 'After picking up the object, you even

went on searching in the mud for some time, in case any coin might have fallen out.'

The old fellow was speechless with anger and fright. 'Some people will say anything at all against an honest man. It's all lies.'

But the Mayor did not believe him, and Master Malandain was brought before him. The man repeated his accusation, and the two cursed each other for an hour. At his own request, Master Hauchecorne was searched, and nothing was found on him.

Finally the Mayor, not knowing what to do, sent him away, warning him that he was going to report the matter to higher authority and ask for instructions.

The news had spread. As he left the Town Hall, the old fellow was surrounded and questioned. And he began to tell the story of the piece of string. No one believed him; they all merely laughed.

As he walked on, everybody stopped him; and he stopped his friends, beginning his story over and over again, declaring his innocence and turning out his pockets to show that he had got nothing.

But everybody said, 'Nonsense, you cunning old devil!'

And he lost his temper because no one would believe him. He did not know what to do but merely went on repeating his story.

It was getting dark, and time to be going home. He set out with three neighbours, to whom he pointed out the spot where he had picked up the piece of string. He talked of it all the way home.

In the evening he took a walk round the village of Bréauté in order to tell everyone. Not one of the people believed a word. He could not sleep all night because he was so worried.

Next day, about one o'clock in the afternoon, Marius Paumelle, a peasant from Ymauville, brought back the wallet with its contents untouched to Master Houlbrèque at Manneville.

The man stated that he had actually found the wallet on the

44

road, but not knowing how to read, had taken it home with him and given it to his employer.

The news soon spread. Master Hauchecorne heard about it, and immediately went round repeating his story with its new ending. He was now proved innocent.

'What annoyed me,' he said, 'wasn't the thing itself, but the lies. Nothing hurts so much as to be blamed because someone has told a lie.'

He talked all day about his adventure. He told the story to people he passed on the road, to people in the inn, and to the people who came out of church. He stopped total strangers to tell them. His mind was now at rest, but something nevertheless still worried him without his knowing exactly what it was. People seemed amused as they listened to him. They didn't seem to believe, and he sometimes heard whispering behind his back.

The following Tuesday he went to the Goderville market simply in order to tell his story.

Malandain, standing at his door, burst out laughing as he passed. He wondered why.

He stopped a farmer from Criquetot, who did not let him finish his story, but shouted at him, 'Nonsense, you cunning old devil,' and walked away.

Master Hauchecorne was still puzzled and was getting more and more worried. Why did they call him 'a cunning old devil'?

At dinner at Jourdain's inn he began again explaining what had happened. A horse-dealer from Montivilliers shouted at him, 'Nonsense, you old devil! I know all about your little games with your string.'

Hauchecorne said uncertainly, 'But the wallet has been found.'

The other replied sharply, 'Shut your mouth, old man. The person who returns a thing isn't always the one who found it.'

The peasant was astonished; at last he understood. He was

being accused of persuading a friend to take the wallet back. He tried to protest, but the whole table roared with laughter.

He could not finish his meal, and went out amid general mocking laughter.

He went home ashamed and indignant, full of rage. He was all the more distressed because, with his Norman cunning, he was quite capable of doing what they thought he had done; and he was capable of boasting about it as a clever trick. His cunning was well known, and he realized that he would never be able to establish his innocence. And the injustice of the suspicion wounded him deeply.

Then he began telling the story all over again, making it longer every day, and adding fresh arguments at every telling. He could never get the incident of the piece of string out of his mind. And the more complicated his defence became, the less did people believe him.

'That's just the sort of argument a fellow uses when he's lying,' people were saying behind his back. He felt it. He was exhausting himself in vain attempts to establish his innocence.

He began to get weaker. The local people used to get him to tell the story of the string for a joke, as people encourage an old soldier to tell the story of his battles.

His mind, seriously affected, was giving way, and towards the end of December he took to his bed.

He died early in January, and in his last fever he kept on protesting that he was innocent, repeating over and over again, 'A little piece of string . . . just a little piece of string, sir . . . look, here it is!'

The Beast

JAKOB WASSERMANN

Jakob Wassermann (1873–1934) was born in Bavaria but lived
mostly in Austria. He wrote novels, short stories, an autobiography, and a life of Columbus. Much of his work had, as a
background, the life of great cities, and he was interested in social
problems. This short story describes what happened during a riot
in a city.

IN one of the former capitals of central Germany great labour
riots, which the citizens still remember with horror, broke out
after a revolution. Thousands of striking labourers gathered and
marched, on that misty February morning, towards the busy
streets of the inner city. Others who were usually idle joined
them, and the police were soon unable to deal with the threatening crowd. The iron shutters came down over the shop-windows;
cafés and restaurants were locked in fear and haste; house doors
were slammed to; and curious and terrified faces appeared at the
windows when the wild shouting and whistling of the approaching crowds could be heard.

Nothing could stop the crowd. Stones were thrown at the
houses and smashed the windows. Here and there a shot was fired.
The police had to take the necessary measures and prepared to
resist the mob with their swords. The noise increased with every
passing moment; the shouts and yells sounded more and more
horrible. Bare arm were stretched forth; eyes burned with hatred.
Women urged the men forward and ragged children filled

the air with screams. Murder and plundering were not far away.

At that moment there drove across a public square which the front of the crowd had just reached a fairly large wagon which resembled a furniture van. But its walls, instead of being made of wood, consisted of loose brown canvas hangings which showed the coat-of-arms of the royal family which had ruled over the country until recently. This hateful sight changed the anger of the rioters into absolute fury. In an instant the wagon was surrounded, and all the efforts of the police to break through the human ring were useless. The driver had stopped the two horses and they were trembling violently.

A man jumped from the back of the wagon, took a rifle from his shoulder, and prepared to fire. This was the signal for the attack. A well-aimed blow knocked him down; and thirty or forty arms reached for the cloth forming the side of the van. The driver's violent and threatening gestures remained unnoticed, and a word which he hurled at them was unheard in the great noise. The protecting canvas cover fell away in bits from the framework.

No sooner had this happened than all, even the boldest of them, were seized with the utmost horror. The whistling, screaming and howling stopped as if by command. Those in the front, who could see the sight, subdued by their horrified silence those at the back, who were only dimly conscious of something terrible; for all they could see with their frightened eyes were the necks in front of them.

On the wagon was a Nubian lion from the royal zoological gardens. The cost of feeding this beast was high and so the new government had decided to sell it to a foreign country. There was also a certain feeling against the playthings of their former lords, and this strengthened the decision. And thus, on that very morning, the lion had been sent to the railway station to set out for its new home.

As the canvas-wall slipped down from the frame, the lion roused himself and then regarded the thousands of people so steadily, and with such majesty, that no sound could be heard from them, not a breath was audible. In the lion's flashing eyes was reflected the picture of a strange world, a world as hard and cold as stone, a world with no horizon, a world of mysterious sounds and unpleasant smells. Did he have an idea of the wild passions which burst forth from despair and misery, he, who knew neither despair nor misery? Did he actually see those ugly faces before him? Or was it only a partial impression of teeth, forehead, chin or angry glance?

But those people out there felt something entirely unknown to him. In the dirty holes where they lived, where their sick ones were lying and where their children were born, they gave way to gloomy thoughts over their injustices. On all their ways and journeys, and in all the dreams of their imaginations they never had a vision that reminded them of the greatness and the might of Nature. It lay beyond their world.

Horror took possession of their souls. They trembled; their muscles became limp; they bowed their heads and cast down their eyes. Gaps opened here and there in the crowd.

The police were able to arrest several dangerous leaders of the strike, and for the time being the rebellion was stopped.

The Sphinx without a Secret

OSCAR WILDE

Oscar Fingal O'Flahertie Wills Wilde (1854–1900) was educated
at Dublin and Oxford. He published poems, novels and plays.
He was sent to prison in 1895 and then wrote the *Ballad of Reading
Gaol* (1898), which is considered by some to be his best work.

The Sphinx without a Secret is about a woman who tried to make
herself mysterious.

ONE afternoon I was sitting outside the Café de la Paix, watching
the splendour and the shabbiness of Parisian life, and wondering
over my drink at the strange view of pride and poverty that
was passing before me, when I heard someone call my name.
I turned round and saw Lord Murchison.

We had not met since we had been at college together, nearly
ten years before, so I was delighted to meet him again, and we
shook hands warmly. At Oxford we had been great friends. I
had liked him immensely: he was so handsome, so high-spirited
and so honourable. We used to say of him that he would be the
best of fellows if he did not always speak the truth, but I think
we really admired him all the more for his frankness.

I found him a good deal changed. He looked anxious and
puzzled, and seemed to be in doubt about something. I felt it
could not be politics, and concluded that it was a woman. So I
asked him if he was married yet.

'I don't understand women well enough,' he answered.

'My dear Gerald,' I said, 'women were meant to be loved, not
to be understood.'

'I cannot love where I cannot trust,' he replied.

'I believe you have a mystery in your life, Gerald,' I exclaimed. 'Tell me about it.'

'Let us go for a drive,' he answered. 'It is too crowded here. No, not a yellow carriage: any other colour—there, that dark green one will do'; and in a few moments we were on our way in the direction of the Madeleine.

'Where shall we go to?' I said.

'Oh, anywhere you like!' he answered—'to the restaurant in the Bois. We will dine there and you shall tell me about yourself.'

'I want to hear about you first,' I said. 'Tell me your mystery.'

He took a little case from his pocket and handed it to me. I opened it. Inside there was the photograph of a woman, tall and slight, with large vague eyes and loose hair.

'What do you think of that face?' he said. 'Is it truthful?'

I examined it carefully. It seemed to me the face of someone who had a secret, but whether the secret was good or evil I could not say. The faint smile that just played across the lips was far too subtle to be really sweet.

'Well,' he cried impatiently, 'what do you say?'

'She has a secret smile,' I said. 'Tell me about her.'

'Not now,' he said. 'After dinner.'

When the waiter brought us our coffee and cigarettes I reminded Gerald of his promise. He walked two or three times up and down the room and, sinking into an armchair, told me the following story.

'One evening,' he said, 'I was walking down Bond Street about five o'clock. There was a terrific crush of carriages, and the traffic was almost stopped. Close to the footpath was standing a little yellow carriage which, for some reason, attracted my attention. As I passed by, there looked out from it the face I showed you this afternoon. I could not forget it. All that night I kept thinking of it, and all the next day. I wandered up and down the

51

roads looking into every carriage and waiting for the yellow one. But I could not find my beautiful unknown, and at last I began to think she was merely a dream.

'About a week afterwards I was dining with Madame de Rastail. Dinner was for eight o'clock, but at half-past eight we were still waiting in the drawing-room. Finally the servant threw open the door and announced Lady Alroy. It was the woman I had been looking for.

'To my intense delight I was asked to take her in to dinner. After we had sat down I remarked quite innocently, "I think I saw you in Bond Street some time ago, Lady Alroy." She grew very pale and said to me in a low voice, "Please do not talk so loud. Someone may hear you." I felt miserable at having made such a bad beginning and started to talk wildly about French plays. She spoke very little and always seemed afraid that someone might be listening. I fell stupidly in love, and the mystery around her made me very curious. When she was going away, I asked if I might call and see her. She hesitated for a moment, glanced round to see if anyone was near us, and then said, "Yes; tomorrow at a quarter to five."

'I begged Madame de Rastail to tell me about her, but all that I could learn was that she was a widow with a beautiful house in Park Lane.

'The next day I arrived at Park Lane punctual to the moment, but was told that Lady Alroy had just gone out. I went to the club unhappy and puzzled, and then wrote her a letter asking if I might come some other afternoon.

'I had no answer for several days, but at last I got a note saying she would be at home on Sunday at four, and with this extraordinary ending: "Please do not write to me here again; I will explain when I see you."

'On Sunday she received me and was perfectly charming; but when I was going away she begged me, if I ever wrote to her again, to address my letter to Mrs. Knox, care of Whittaker's Library, Green Street. "There are reasons," she said, "why I cannot receive letters in my own house."

'All through the season I saw her a great deal, and the atmosphere of mystery never left her. Sometimes I thought she was in the power of some man, but I could not really believe it. It was very difficult for me to come to any conclusion, but at last I determined to ask her to become my wife. I was sick and tired of the unending secrecy. I wrote to her at the library to ask her if she could see me the following Monday at six. She answered yes, and I was in the seventh heaven of delight. I loved her; but the mystery troubled me, maddened me. But chance helped me.'

'You discovered it, then?'

'I fear so,' he answered. 'You can judge for yourself.

'When Monday came I went to lunch with my uncle, who, as you know, lives in Regent's Park. I wanted to reach Piccadilly and took a short cut through a lot of shabby little streets. Suddenly I saw in front of me Lady Alroy, deeply veiled and walking very fast. On coming to the last house in the street, she went up the steps, took out a key and let herself in.

' "Here is the mystery," I said to myself; and I hurried on and examined the house. It seemed a sort of place for lodgings. On the doorstep lay her handkerchief, which she had dropped. I picked it up and put it in my pocket. Then I began to consider what I should do. I drove to the club and at six I called to see her.

'She was lying on a sofa, beautifully dressed and looking very lovely. "I am so glad to see you," she said; "I have not been out all day." I stared at her in amazement and, pulling the handkerchief out of my pocket, handed it to her. "You dropped this in Cumnor Street this afternoon, Lady Alroy," I said very calmly.

'She looked at me in terror, but made no attempt to take the handkerchief. "What were you doing there?" I asked.

' "What right have you to question me?" she said.

On coming to the last house in the street, she went up the steps.

54

' "The right of the man who loves you," I replied. "I came here to ask you to be my wife." She hid her face in her hands and burst into a flood of tears. "You must tell me," I said.

'She stood up, and looking me straight in the face, said, "Lord Murchison, there is nothing to tell you."

' "You went to meet someone," I cried. "That is your mystery."

'She grew dreadfully white, and said, "I went to meet no one."

' "Can't you tell the truth?" I exclaimed.

' "I have told it," she replied.

'I was mad; I don't know what I said, but I said terrible things to her. Finally I rushed out of the house. She wrote me a letter the next day; I sent it back unopened. Then I went to Norway, and when I came back after a month the first thing I saw in the paper was the death of Lady Alroy. She had caught a chill at the Opera and had died five days later. I shut myself up and saw no one. I had loved her so much, I had loved her so madly.'

'You went to the street, to the house in it?' I asked.

'Yes,' he answered. 'One day I went to Cumnor Street, and a respectable-looking woman opened the door of the house. She told me that the drawing-rooms were let to a lady. "But I have not seen her for three months," she said.

' "Is this the lady?" I asked, showing her the photograph.

' "Yes, sir," she said. "When is she coming back?"

' "The lady is dead," I said. "Did she meet anyone when she came here?"

'But the woman assured me that it was not so, that she always came alone and saw no one. "She simply sat in the drawing-room, sir, reading books, and sometimes had tea."

'I did not know what to say, so I gave her some money and left. Now, what do you think it all meant? You don't believe the woman was telling the truth?'

'I do.'

'Then why did Lady Alroy go there?'

'My dear Gerald,' I answered, 'Lady Alroy was simply a woman who madly desired to have a mystery. She took those rooms for the pleasure of going there with her veil down, and imagining herself a heroine. She was only a Sphinx without a secret.'

'Do you really think so?' he asked.

'I am sure of it.'

He took out the case, opened it, and looked at the photograph. 'I wonder,' he said.

The Orderly

EDMONDO DE AMICIS

Edmondo de Amicis (1846–1908) was born in Liguria and chose
the army as his profession. He fought at the second battle of
Custozza (1866) and then began to write about army life. He left
the army in 1870 and travelled widely. His descriptions of
London, Spain, Holland and Morocco are important.

   The short story given below is concerned with life in the army
during the nineteenth century in Italy.

FOR the past four years they had been together, and never for an
instant had either forgotten that one was the officer, the other the
soldier. The officer was militarily severe, the soldier obedient.
And they were fond of each other with that rough, silent affection
which does not show itself, but hides a burst of tenderness beneath a hard action, eloquent when it is silent, and accustomed to
bite the lips and repress any tears in order not to appear weak.
They used few words and understood each other with a glance
or a gesture.

   'Lieutenant, have you any further orders for me?'
   'No.'
   'May I go?'
   'Go.'
This was the daily method of dismissal. Never another word.
And thus months and years—four years—had passed, in camp, at
home, in war, in exercises. And gradually there had grown in
each heart, but scarcely suspected by them, a stern affection for
the other.

They had found themselves side by side on the battlefield, a hundred paces from the enemy's cannon, and each time a shell had whistled past their ears, one had glanced round swiftly to seek the other, and seeing him had given a sigh of relief, thinking, 'We've escaped again.' Together they had stood guard more than one cold and rainy night, their feet in the mud, the wind slapping their faces; and when the relief guard arrived they had exchanged a smile, as if to say, 'Now we are going back to camp. Cheer up. You'll be able to rest.'

After such moments of freedom, they had returned to their habitual silent and severe manner. Not once had the soldier forgotten to raise his hand to his cap when meeting or leaving his officer, raising his head and looking him straight in the eye.

They had been together for four years; but now the soldier was about to be discharged. One day the officer commanding had received orders to discharge the group to which the orderly belonged.

That day the officer and the soldier exchanged only a few more than the ordinary number of words, but their hearts spoke at great length.

'Have you any further orders?'

'Nothing. The order for your discharge has arrived; in ten days you will leave.'

A brief silence followed, and their eyes did not meet.

'May I go?'

'Go, if you wish.'

These few additional words represented a great step along the road to tenderness. One was about to lose a friend—even more than a friend, a brother. The other too, without doubt, was about to lose a friend, but he at least was returning home.

For him this thought was a great comfort. To return home! After so many years, so many perils. How often in camp he had thought of his mother: 'What is the poor woman doing now?'

58

How often he had heard those tunes that he used to sing at home! To return home! To return unexpectedly and see again the country and the houses, recognize a roof from a distance, arrive breathless, see his little sister grown up, his brother a young man. The very thought of these things was sufficient to sweeten any bitterness, and heal any wound.

But the brave fellow could not reconcile himself to the idea of being obliged to leave his officer. And a soldier never removes his worn coat, which has served him for a cover and pillow for so many years, without a certain feeling of heart-break, as if he were about to forsake a friend. Those back pockets in which, while in prison, he used to hide his pipe at the approach of the officer of the guard, and for which, from force of habit, he still searches with his hands . . . How vexing not to find them any longer!

The officer and the soldier did not add to their usual words, but they caught each other's eye more frequently, seeming to say, 'You are suffering, I know.' The soldier performed his duties with less haste, in order to remain as long as possible in the officer's house. He pretended to dust the tables and chairs, but more often, lost in his sad thoughts, he moved his duster in space without touching anything. Meanwhile, the officer, erect and motionless, with arms crossed, attentively followed the soldier's steps.

'Lieutenant, may I go?'

'Go.'

And the soldier left.

He had scarcely gone down two steps when there came a sudden call from the room: 'Come here,' and he returned.

'Have you any further orders?'

'No. I merely wished to say . . . nothing, nothing; you can do it tomorrow. Go.'

Perhaps he had called him back simply to see him.

Finally the day for departure arrived. The officer was smoking, and the smoke brought tears to his eyes. In half an hour the orderly would come to take his leave definitely. The officer sat and thought, 'I ought to have been prepared for this departure. Didn't I know that I couldn't keep him for ever? Wasn't I aware that his term of service was five years? The man has a home where he was born and has grown up, a family that he left with sorrow and will now rejoin with joy. Why should he stay with me? What does he owe to me? I have always been severe towards him. It's my character. I am unable to find the proper words—and in the army one dare not utter them. I can at least show him a more human face . . . And now he is going away, after so many years of companionship. But that's our life, and one must reconcile oneself to it. What a good fellow! A heart of gold! If sometimes, while marching, overcome by fatigue, burnt by the sun, choked by the dust, I stopped a moment and glanced round as if to search for a little water, instantly a cup was handed to me and a voice close at my side said, "Do you want a drink, Lieutenant?"

'It was he. He had secretly left the march, had run to get water far away, who knows where? He had returned rapidly, streaming with sweat, exhausted, and waited behind me until I expressed a desire to drink. In camp, if I fell asleep in the shade of a tree, and the sun gradually began to beat on my face, a hand arranged the branches above me, or spread a cloak over a stack of arms to shield me from the sun. It was he, always he. And in camp he brought straw and spread it on the grass; he piled it at one end as a pillow and said, "Is that all right, Lieutenant?"

' "Good fellow," I thought then. "Go," I said. "Go and rest, for you need it."

' "But will that do?" he said. "If it is not enough, I'll go and fetch some more."

' "Yes, yes. This will do. Go and rest, go. Do not lose any more time."

'And during a march at night, if I were seized by sleep and

walked about staggering from one side of the road to the other, and approached too near a ditch, a light hand was placed on my arm and pushed me gently towards the middle of the road, and a timid voice murmured, "Look out, Lieutenant, there is a ditch." Always he! What had I done that he should always treat me with such attention and affection? I am selfish. I think only of myself. I am convinced he would give his life for me. For what reason has this poor fellow with rough face and hands, with body toughened by suffering, without education, become as timid and gentle as a maiden? He holds his breath so as not to disturb my sleep. It is certain that the human heart learns under these clothes new feelings unknown to him who has never been a soldier. People think that the only feelings we have are those that we feel in war. How little they know us! The heart of a soldier never grows old; it keeps the affections of youth. To understand the companionship of the army, you must have passed many nights in camp, or have made long marches in the heat of summer, have been on guard in lashing rain, have suffered hunger and thirst to the point of fainting, and in all these circumstances have had a friend at your side who has placed his cloak over you to protect you from the cold, has brought you a little water or bread and deprived himself. Servant? Such a man a servant? It is wicked to describe him thus' (exclaims our officer, with a passionate wave of his hand).

'This faithful companion is to leave me, and I shall see him no more. No! Impossible! I will go to see him when he goes home. I know the name of his town. I will ask the way to his village and his farm. I will surprise him in the fields and call him by name. "Don't you remember your officer?" "Whom do I see? Lieutenant? You here!" he will reply, overcome with emotion. "Yes, I had to see you!" I will say. "Come here, my good soldier." '

The officer was occupied with these thoughts when he heard a light, slow, unequal step on the stairs, like that of a person who cannot advance without hesitation. He listened without turning his head. The step approached. There was a clutching at his heart. He turned. There he was. There was the orderly. He!

He looked worried and his eyes were red. He saluted, took a step forward, stopped and regarded his officer. The latter turned his head away.

'Lieutenant, I'm going.'

'Farewell,' replied the officer, pressing his lips together and continuing to look in the other direction. 'Farewell. A pleasant journey . . . return home . . . work . . . continue to live like a good fellow, just as you've done until now, and . . . good-bye.'

'Lieutenant!' exclaimed the soldier in a trembling voice, taking a step towards him.

'Go, go, or you will be late. Go. It's late already. Hurry.'

And he extended a hand that the soldier pressed firmly. 'A pleasant journey . . . and remember me. Think of your officer sometimes.'

The poor fellow wanted to reply, tried to form a word with his mouth, but could only groan. He still gripped the hand, looked at the officer, whose head was still turned away, advanced a step . . . 'Ah, Lieutenant!' he cried.

Then he fled.

The other, remaining alone, turned round, gazed for a short time at the door and then rested his elbows on the table and sank his head in his hands. Two large tears formed in his eyes and slipped swiftly down his cheeks, as if afraid of being seen. He passed his hand over his eyes and looked at his cigar. It was out.

He let his head fall on his arm and abandoned himself to grief.

Mirrors

MASSIMO BONTEMPELLI

Massimo Bontempelli was born at Como in 1878, took to writing and tried every form of literary expression. His volumes of short stories probably include his best work. This story, *Mirrors*, is taken from the volume, *La Donna dei Miei Sogni*,* and is written in a mood of light laughter.

It is necessary that I describe one of my experiences with mirrors. I know that I shall be blamed, but patience, my friend. I would prefer not to have some evil person think that I spend most of my life before a mirror. On the contrary I seldom use this object; and therefore it creates for me the strange ideas that do not come to those who make of it too ordinary an article of use.

About eight days ago, on a morning towards noon, my land-lady woke me up with a telegram. After a few willing efforts, I managed to put myself into a condition to read it. It was a telegram from Vienna. It was addressed to me, to me alone, and it was correctly addressed. This is what it said:

'Leave for Rome day after tomorrow stop arrivederci† stop Massimo.'

I was in Vienna two months ago for fifteen days. I tried to remember all the persons I had met there during those fifteen days. There was an old Hungarian friend of mine called Tibor, and some others named Fritz, Richard and John. I thought and

* The Lady of my Dreams.
† Au revoir! Till we meet again!

thought again, but I could think of no other Massimo in Vienna but myself.

There was just one conclusion and it was a clear one. Since I was the only Massimo I could think of in Vienna, the Massimo who sent me that telegram was myself.

It was my telegram, therefore.

'I understand!' —I shouted.

But the reader, on the other hand, cannot yet have understood.

I shall explain. But before I do so it is necessary that I tell my reader about some of the other experiences that I have had in this matter of telegrams. A single example will be enough. I was arranging my belongings in my room one day when I noticed that my umbrella was gone. I looked for it everywhere. More than once (as we are in the habit of doing in such cases, as if once were not enough) I looked for it in the corner where I usually kept it, but in vain. I finally accepted the loss and went about my business: we lose greater things in life than an umbrella.

I had almost forgotten it when, two days later, I received the following telegram: 'Shall arrive tonight Umbrella.' I gave it little thought and at night I went to bed peacefully. The following morning the first thing to attract my attention was my umbrella. Sure enough, there it was, in the very corner where I had looked for it many times.

Of course, I know perfectly well that it is not an uncommon thing (even if science has not yet explained it) to find a lost article in the very place where one has looked for it many times before. And there is really no use in talking about it. But when a lost article announces its return by telegram, that is not so common.

With this example in mind, the thing that struck me in reading that telegram from Vienna, and which I am about to explain, ought to seem quite natural even to the most practical of my readers.

But here we have to go back a bit.

64

Two months ago in Vienna I was standing before a mirror fixing my tie. I was getting ready to take my train back to Rome. There were political demonstrations going on throughout the city at the time.

As I have said, I was standing before a mirror fixing my tie. Suddenly a tremendous explosion shook the house and smashed my mirror to bits.

I realized it was a bomb, and I went on fixing my tie without a mirror. When I was ready I took my bag, drove to the station, and left. A few days later I was in Rome. It was late at night, so I immediately undressed and went to bed.

The next morning I stood before my mirror with my shaving brush in one hand and a towel in the other, when to my great surprise I saw nothing there. To be more exact, there was everything there but me. I could see a soapy brush and an agitated towel. But I? I was not to be seen. Neither my face nor my image was there.

Realizing at once what had happened, I broke into laughter.

All those who use a mirror, the women especially, must have noticed that the moment they pull themselves away from it, from the mirror into which they are looking, they feel a slight sense of discomfort. There is a little jerk at the parting. Well, this results from the very light effort we all make when tearing ourselves away, when withdrawing the image that is there.

Now what happened to me on that day in Vienna? My mirror broke so instantly, it was smashed and destroyed so suddenly, that I was not quick enough to withdraw my image, to pull it back before it vanished.

Naturally, as I was in a hurry, I paid little attention to the incident at the time. I first realized what had happened when I found myself facing a mirror here in Rome two days later, as I have said.

And so for these past two months I have been without my

To my great surprise I saw nothing there.

image. It was rather troublesome at first, but I learned to get on without it. I took the mirror down from its usual place and put it away in my trunk.

The only thing I had to be very careful about was not to let anyone see me standing before any of the mirrors along the streets, in the cafés, or in the homes of others. People are easily surprised, you know. They would want to know why and how, and then I should have to explain. This would be annoying.

For this reason, though the loss itself was not very serious, I was happy to receive that telegram eight days ago. I understood at once (and by this time I suppose all my readers have understood) that the telegram had been sent to me by my own image so that I might be informed of its homecoming.

Naturally I did not hasten to look at myself in the mirror. Not at all. I did not want to give my image the satisfaction of knowing that I care very much about it, that I have been waiting for it impatiently, that I cannot do without it. It left Vienna eight days ago, and it should have reached here at least four days ago. But I did not show myself until yesterday. It was only yesterday that I went to get the mirror from my trunk, whistling a tune from *Aida* as I did so. I restored it to its place in the bathroom without even looking at it. Then with the calmest indifference I arranged my collar and tie and took a glimpse at myself. There I was! There was my image, not changed at all. I had had a vague fear that I might find it a little disturbed, somewhat angry about my indifference, and probably tired from the long trip and its many experiences. Instead, it seemed to be in the finest condition, and as indifferent and calm as its owner.

The House of a Black Dog

SATO HARUO

Sato Haruo is one of the modern Japanese writers, and was born in 1892. This story about a walk with a dog was first published in 1916, and is translated by George Saito. Although slight, it carries the reader along from one incident to another, so that he finds it difficult to stop reading before he reaches the end.

FRATE starts running suddenly and waits for me at the parting of the road. He is a very clever dog and has been my friend for years. I am convinced that he is far cleverer than most men, not to mention my wife. So I take Frate with me whenever I go for a walk. Sometimes he leads me to some quite unexpected spot. That is why, when I go for a walk now, I do not have any fixed destination, but follow obediently wherever my dog leads me. So far I have never been down the side-street and so I shall follow the dog there.

The narrow road is on a gentle slope which occasionally makes sharp twists. I walk along behind my dog, not looking at the scenery, nor thinking. Now and then I look up and observe the clouds in the sky. Suddenly some flowers by the roadside catch my attention. I pick a few and hold them to my nose. I do not know what they are called but they smell good. I walk along, twisting them between my fingers. Frate happens to notice them. He stops for a moment, tilts his head to the side and gazes into my eyes. He sniffs at the flowers, and glances up at me as if to say that he wishes they were dog biscuits. Then he starts running down the road once more.

I walk along like this for nearly two hours. We seem to be climbing considerably and soon I can see quite a good view. Below the open fields that stretch out before me I can vaguely see some town in the distance between the mist and the clouds. I stand there for some time gazing at it. Yes, it is certainly a town. But what town can possibly be lying there with all those houses? There is something rather peculiar about the whole scene. I am totally ignorant about the geography of these parts, however, and there is really nothing surprising about seeing an unfamiliar town. I look down the other side of the hill. It slopes down gently into the distance. The entire surface is covered with dense thickets. It is a short time before noon and the gentle spring sun shines like smoke, like scent, through the fresh green leaves. The balance of the shade and the sun on the tree-trunks and on the ground is beautiful beyond words. I want to go into the depths of that forest.

My friend Frate seems to be thinking the same. He advances merrily into the forest and I follow him. When we have gone a little more than a hundred yards, the dog begins to walk in a different way. He abandons his easy walk and moves his legs forward busily. He thrusts his nose forward. He must have found something. For a few moments he hurries to and fro restlessly. Then he seems to find the right path and walks straight ahead. My curiosity is slightly aroused and I follow him. From time to time we startle the wild birds in the branches.

After we have walked along at a rapid pace for about half an hour, Frate suddenly comes to a halt. At the same moment I seem to hear running water. Jerking his ears irritably, Frate walks back a few yards, sniffs the ground once again, and then sets off to the left. I am surprised to find how deep the forest is. There must be 700 acres of woods.

My dog's peculiar behaviour fills me with curiosity. After another half hour of walking, Frate stops again and barks. Now

I see that a house is standing directly in front of me. There is something very strange about it. Why should anyone have a house in a place like this?

A quick glance tells me that there is no garden. The house has clearly been built in such a position that it can only be seen when one is standing directly before it. As I walk closer, I see that it is quite an ordinary sort of house, but at the same time it is rather hard to say exactly what type of house it is. It is not an ordinary farm-house. The windows have glass in them, in the Western style. I cannot see an entrance, and so I suppose I must be facing the back or the side.

Whatever happens I must go in and have a look inside. I can say that I have lost my way. No doubt they will offer me a cup of tea, and Frate and I will eat the lunch that I have brought with me in a box.

With this in mind I walk to the front of the house, and suddenly I hear a stream near by. When I reach the front, I find that, like the rest of the house, it directly faces the forest. There is one peculiar thing about it, however: it is far more luxuriously built than the other parts of the building. Four fine stone steps lead up to the front door. This stone is far older than the remainder of the house.

The house faces south and beneath the front window a row of small red roses grows along the wall. From under them flows a stream of water glittering brightly in the sun. At first glance it looks as if the water were flowing out of the house itself. My friend Frate starts drinking the water eagerly; he evidently finds it delicious.

Now I quietly walk up the steps. I can clearly hear the sound of my shoes against the stone, but they do not really disturb the quiet of the surrounding scene. I wonder if I am visiting the house of a magician. I look round and see Frate standing there carelessly with his pink tongue hanging out and his tail wagging.

In the Western manner I knock on the Western-style door. There is no answer. I have to knock again. Still no answer. This time I call out, 'May I come in?' There is not the slightest result. Is the owner out, I wonder, or is the house completely unoccupied? A strange feeling comes over me. I go to the front window where the roses are growing—for some reason I walk as quietly as possible—and standing on my toes I look inside the house.

The window has a heavy dark curtain decorated with blue lines. Obviously of very good quality, it does not suit the rest of the house. The curtain has been partly pulled aside and I can see into the room. To my surprise I find a large stone basin, about two feet high, standing in the middle of the room. Water is gushing up from the centre of the basin and pouring constantly over the sides. The floor, too, is of stone and it looks rather damp. (When I think about it later, I realize that the water running over the edge of the basin is the same glittering water that I saw gliding like a snake from among the roses.)

The basin really amazes me. Although I have felt from the beginning that there is something peculiar about the house, I never expected to find such a strange thing inside. I become more curious and I start carefully examining the inside of the house through the window.

The floor is made of some pale stone whose name I do not know. Round the basin where it is wet it has taken on a beautiful blue colour. On the wall furthest from the entrance there is a stone fireplace and to the right three bookshelves with dishes piled on the top. Near the window is a desk, and on the desk, yes, what is it on the desk? It is a cigarette-end, and from it gently rises a thread of smoke. Someone must have been here a moment ago.

I light a cigarette myself and make up my mind that I must go into the house. If the owner happens to be out and comes back and finds me inside, I'll explain my reason honestly. Once again

I can see into the room.

I climb the steps to the entrance and call, 'Is anyone there?' No answer. Quietly I open the door. It is unlocked.

As soon as I have walked in, I draw back. For there, lying in the sun under the window, is a coal-black Spanish dog, who has been sleeping with his chin on the floor. When he hears me he stands up slowly.

Frate starts growling and walks up to the black dog. For a time they growl at each other, and then the Spanish dog starts wagging his tail. Then he lies down in the same place as before. Frate lies down beside him. I feel happier and walk into the room.

The Spanish dog looks old. He is very big and I pat his head. Dogs in lonely places will never hurt people who are nice to them; and the Spanish dog now happily licks my hand.

But who and where is the owner of the house? I am free to examine the place from top to bottom but I feel anxious and stand by the large stone basin. No doubt the people who live here use this water for drinking.

In the room there are three chairs—one by the basin, one by the fireplace, and one by a table. I can hear a clock. Where can it be? Ah, yes, there it is on the table. And there is the cigarette that I saw from outside. But it is now completely burnt.

There is an old-world picture on the clock, and I notice that the clock itself is slow. It says a quarter past one: it is one hour slow. There are some German books—rather dusty—and a picture on the wall.

I decide to leave the house and go home. Perhaps I'll call again one of these days and meet the real owner, not the dog. But I feel rather anxious—perhaps I ought to wait until the owner comes back. I watch the water gushing out of the basin and light another cigarette. I seem to hear some sort of music coming from the distance. I listen with admiration. Can it be coming from the water?

I go to the door and whistle for Frate. The Spanish dog, who seems to have been watching every movement, now gazes at me as I prepare to leave. I become frightened. Perhaps that dog has only been pretending to be gentle, and now that he sees me going he may jump on me from behind and bite me. I wait impatiently for Frate to follow me; then I hurry out of the door, carefully watching the Spanish dog, and shut it with a bang.

Before setting out for home, I decide to have a final glance inside the house. I stand on my toes at the window and look in. The Spanish dog gets slowly to his feet and walks towards the table.

'Well, that was quite a startling visit I had today,' he seems to say to himself in a human voice, evidently unaware of my presence. He yawns in the way that dogs often do—and then suddenly he becomes a middle-aged man in glasses and a black suit who stands leaning against the chair by the table with a still unlit cigarette in his mouth, and who slowly turns the pages of one of those books.

It is a very warm spring afternoon. I am in a thicket of trees among the silent hills.

The Cup of Tea

AFFONSO BOTELHO

The short story has been less developed in Portuguese than in any other Latin literature; moreover, the Portuguese, when they write a story, rarely make it a comic one. But *The Cup of Tea*, written in the nineteenth century, breaks this rule. It is a care-free story of a traveller who was determined, in spite of all obstacles, to get a cup of tea, and it describes the difficulties that he met as he pursued his object.

NOT very many years ago the journey from Oporto to Regoa had to be made partly by stage-coach and partly by rail, as the country permitted.

The stage-coach, drawn by six powerful horses, stood at the point of departure from the offices of the Coaching Company in Oporto, awaiting the final arrivals. In the wild crowd around the coach, some passengers declared that they could not get the places they had booked and others could not find their luggage. The general disturbance was penetrated from time to time by the rough language of the porters.

A young man sat in one of the places near the door. He had taken his seat early, and his luggage was all in order. The other places were all filled with the exception of the one opposite him; and this one appeared to be reserved for some passenger who had not been able to arrive in time. The driver gathered up the reins, and the guard began to sound the signal for departure.

Suddenly a strange sight came round the corner—a fat man walking like a duck, breathing hard, and waving an enormous umbrella in the direction of the coach. After him came two porters with a load of luggage.

The guard used some strong language, the luggage was lifted up, and the fat passenger climbed into the empty place. With some difficulty he found room for his umbrella and a big rain-cloak.

The horses set off along the stony streets of Oporto in the direction of the road leading to the railway station of the Minho-Douro line. The fat passenger seemed annoyed about something, for he muttered impatiently to himself, and could not sit still. At last he caught the eye of the young man opposite, João de Sousa.

'It is too bad, sir,' he exclaimed. 'Just think: I could not get my cup of tea!'

João de Sousa did not answer, but looked questioningly at the fat man, who went on:

'You see, it has always been my custom to take a cup of tea after my lunch; just a cup of strong black tea. I was in such a hurry to catch the coach that I did not wait for tea just now. I cannot tell you how I miss it. You see, sir, when a man comes to my age, habits are everything, and it is really dreadful to have to break your habits. Now I know I shall be miserable through-out the journey because I could not have my cup of tea. You are young, sir, but take the advice of a man who is of regular habits. When you once form a steady habit, let nothing put you off it.'

João de Sousa was amused. 'But when we get to the railway station,' he said, 'you will be able to get tea in the refreshment room.'

'Of course! I had not thought of that! It will be a little bit late after my lunch, but at least it will be something.'

When they got to the station, the train was already at the

76

platform. Everyone rushed into the refreshment room to prepare for the train journey, some by drinking a glass of wine and eating some bread and fruit, others by purchasing food to eat in the train.

The fat man sat down at one of the tables and looked round for a waiter. But there were few of them, and it was some time before he attracted the attention of one and ordered a cup of tea. He was about to give details of the tea that he wanted, but the busy waiter had to attend to other orders. At last João de Sousa, when going off to take his place in the train, saw the fat man preparing to enjoy his favourite drink.

Presently he came rushing out and climbed into the train just as the whistle sounded. He sat down opposite João de Sousa, and wiped his face with a brilliant silk handkerchief.

'Well?' João de Sousa smiled.

'My dear boy, it was green tea that the waiter brought me. I can never drink green tea!'

The train passed through the magnificent mountains, past little farm-houses and streams. Night was coming on and the setting sun had gone down below the hills. The fat passenger saw no beauty in the scene. He yawned and uttered impatient exclamations under his breath. De Sousa heard a moan ending with the word 'tea'.

'You can soon have your cup of tea,' he said.

'Where?'

'We leave the train at Cahide and take another stage-coach.'

'Ah, so we do! I had not thought of it. Many thanks for reminding me. I can get tea at the inn where the coach starts.'

The fat passenger then began to sing contentedly to himself until he fell into a heavy sleep, lulled by the motion of the train. He did not open his eyes until João de Sousa gave him a little shake.

'What is it? Where are we?'

'We are at Cahide and we must get out here and take the coach.'

'You are very kind, sir.' The fat man began to gather up his luggage.

Two stage-coaches were standing outside the inn, one on the way to Villa Real and the other to Regoa. Passing the restaurant on his way to the coaches, João de Sousa found the fat passenger arguing violently with a waiter. He stopped to ask if he was going to Regoa or to Villa Real.

'I am going to Regoa, sir. Just think of it! A terrible thing! I cannot get my cup of tea.'

'That is a very serious matter indeed,' said the young man gravely.

'Serious? I believe you. What sort of a restaurant is this? There is not a leaf of black tea in the place!'

'All passengers for Regoa take their places, please,' called out the guard, an interesting figure in the old coaching dress of the place.

The fat passenger again sat down opposite João de Sousa.

'So you have been disappointed again, sir?'

'Don't speak of it. It is too awful. What a journey to make without my cup of tea!'

'But you will have another chance in Amarante, where we change the horses.'

'Oh, I am glad. You are very good, sir.'

The coach rolled on through the country roads, and in spite of the motion and the noise the passengers slept. João de Sousa remained awake, watching the country pass under the light of the moon: the trees, the hedges, the lights from the houses of a village on the hillside. Presently they came to the ancient bridge of Amarante, the origin of which is lost in the mists of the past. The coach passed into the narrow stony street, and stopped outside the famous old inn of the Capadeira.

João de Sousa found the fat passenger arguing violently with a waiter.

The dining-room of the inn was full of tobacco smoke and the smell of chocolate. The waiter advanced to show the travellers to their seats, and presently a really excellent supper was served. This João de Sousa thoroughly enjoyed, drinking the good wine of Valdepenas. He looked round and saw the fat passenger sitting at a corner of the table, waiting anxiously to speak to the waiter.

'Waiter, I want a cup of tea, strong and black, remember. No other will do.'

'Sir, in an instant. I must just serve the supper, and then I will order the tea for you. What will you have for supper, sir?'

'I cannot eat anything until I have had my tea.'

The waiter continued serving the great dishes of chicken and all kinds of excellent food; and bottles of good wine were passed merrily round the table. The fat passenger waited patiently. Presently it was announced that the coach would start in five minutes, and there was great excitement and confusion. Everyone rushed to find a place in the coach, and João de Sousa heard the unhappy voice of the fat passenger saying, 'And my tea? Waiter, what about that tea?'

'In one minute, sir.'

All had taken their places except the fat man, who stood at the door of the inn impatiently. As the coach had to climb the mountain for some distance, a strong team of twelve oxen had been fastened to it, gay with red caps and brass bells. The guard called to the fat passenger, 'Take your place, sir, if you please. I can wait no longer.'

Suddenly the waiter came running with a steaming cup of tea on a tray. The fat passenger had one foot on the step of the coach, but he uttered a cry of joy, seized the cup, and raised it to his lips. But the next instant he cried out in distress, and put the cup back on the tray.

'Impossible to drink this tea, waiter. It is boiling hot. Why do you bring it like that, when the coach is just starting?' And he climbed into his place opposite João de Sousa, tears of pain and annoyance in his eyes.

The stage-coach climbed the hill slowly for five hours, dragged by the slow but powerful oxen. A fine rain fell on the enormous old trees beside the mountain road, and the wind whistled through their branches. Here and there little streams ran down from the mountain snows towards the mighty River Douro.

The driver walked beside the leader of the team, encouraging the oxen. All the passengers except João de Sousa slept. They passed a stone-built house near the road, and the moon threw strange reflections on its roof. Higher up they passed a little cottage above which hung a massive block of stone which looked as if it might fall at any moment. The road grew narrower as they approached the top, and the sun rose, bathing the mountain in many colours—purple, pink and yellow. The coach stopped at an inn near the village of Quintella, and those passengers who were awake descended to stretch their legs in the pure morning air.

João de Sousa walked along admiring the splendour of the scenery. Peak after peak extended as far as the eye could see, and lower down shone a wide stretch of water. The whole lovely picture was framed in the great trees, and as the young man paused to draw a breath of delight he heard a slow step approaching. A long yawn of weariness sounded close to his ear, and João de Sousa smiled at the sight of the fat passenger, still half asleep, and so different from the glory of the new morning.

'Well, sir, how are you? What about your tea now?'

'Oh, my dear young friend, I have really lost all hope. There is no tea in that miserable inn; they say no one ever asks for such a thing.'

The horses were ready, and the guard gave the signal for the start. They went fast down the mountain-side and were soon among dark trees and then fruit. Presently the passengers were among the grapes that grow by the Douro. By the side of the great river they drove for many miles until the houses grew thicker and gardens appeared. At last they entered the white streets of Regoa. It was just half past eight in the morning, the right hour for breakfast.

As the coach stopped at the hotel, a fine building with green shutters, the fat passenger turned to João de Sousa with a smile. 'I thank you, sir for all your courtesy. I should have had a dreadful journey indeed without your agreeable company. I cannot tell you how I have suffered from the loss of my cup of tea. It is wrong to give up habits at my age. Take my advice, sir, and do not allow anything to interfere with a habit you have formed, if it is a good one. Now I am at last going to get my cup of tea. It is late, it is true, but better late than never. Permit me to introduce myself, sir. My name is Barnabé dos Anjos; I am a native of the town of Freixo-de-Espada-à-Cinta, and I am travelling to Douro on business. I hope to meet you again, sir, and in any case I am always at your service. I wish you good luck and a safe journey; and now I am going, my dear young friend, to drink your health in a cup of tea.'

The Chameleon

ANTON CHEKHOV

A chameleon is a small animal which changes its colour to suit its surroundings; in this way it avoids danger and is hardly noticed. But Chekhov's chameleon was a policeman.

Anton Chekhov (1860–1904) wrote about the Russian period of depression. He has been compared to Guy de Maupassant in France: he takes a moment in the life of some man and shows the man's character and soul in a few pages. Although Chekhov knew the weaknesses and faults of Russia, he did not find a way out of the troubles. *The Chameleon* is a good and characteristic example of his short stories.

THE police sergeant Achumyelof, wearing his new cloak and with something under his arm, is walking across the market-place. He is followed by a red-haired policeman carrying some confiscated fruit. Quiet reigns all around. Not a soul in the market-place. The open doors and windows of the shops gaze out sadly upon God's world like hungry mouths wide open.

Suddenly Achumyelof hears someone shouting: 'So you want to bite, you accursed beast! Nowadays dogs are not allowed to bite. Stop him! Oh, oh!'

The howling of a dog is heard. Achumyelof looks in the direction from which the sound comes and sees a dog, limping on three legs, run out of Pinchugin's wood-yard. A man in a white shirt is chasing him. The man is close at the dog's heels; suddenly he falls forward to the ground and takes hold of the dog's hind feet. Again the dog's howling is heard and again the cry. Sleepy

83

faces appear at the windows of the shops, and at the wood-yard a crowd quickly gathers as though it had grown out of the ground.

'Do you think it can be a riot?' asks the policeman.

Achumyelof turns to the left and walks towards the crowd. Near the gate of the yard he sees the man in the white shirt holding up his right hand and showing the crowd a bloody finger. On his half-drunken face there is an expression as though he were saying, 'Wait; I will make you pay for this, you devil!' In this man Achumyelof recognizes Khriukin, the goldsmith. In the centre of the crowd, with his forefeet spread out and trembling from head to foot, sits the author of the whole trouble—a young white dog with a yellow spot on his back. In his watery eyes there is an expression of distrust.

'What is the matter?' asks Achumyelof, making his way through the crowd. 'Why are you here? What is the matter with your finger? Who has been screaming?'

'I was just walking along, sir, not touching anybody,' says Khriukin, 'to see about the wood for Dimitri Dimitriyevitch when suddenly this devil of a dog bites my finger. You will excuse me. I am a man who works; I have very particular work to do, and somebody will have to pay me, for I won't be able to use this finger maybe for a week! There is nothing in the law, sir, about having to bear things from animals! If they are all going to bite, it would be better not to live in this world.'

'Now,' says Achumyelof sternly, moving his eyebrows up and down, 'now, whose dog is this? I shall not allow this matter to rest. I will teach you people not to let your dogs run about loose! It is time that something was done about people who won't obey regulations. I will punish the owner. I will show him who I am! Yeldyrin,' turning to the policeman, 'find out whose dog it is and draw up a report. The dog will be killed. Do it quickly. He is probably a mad dog, in any case. Whose dog is it?'

'He looks like General Yigalof's dog,' says someone in the crowd.

'General Yigalof's? Hm! Yeldyrin, take off my cloak; it is terribly hot! It is probably going to rain. There is one thing that I do not understand: how could that dog bite you?' says Achumyelof, turning to Khriukin. 'He does not come up to your fingers. He is such a little dog and you are such a big man. You have probably torn your finger on a nail, and afterwards the idea of the dog occurred to you and you are trying to get some money. I know you people. You are devils!'

'He put a cigarette in the dog's face; but the dog is no fool and bit him, sir.'

'You lie! He did not see it, sir. But let the judge decide. The law says that nowadays we are all equal. I have a brother in the police. If you—'

'Stop talking!'

'No, that is not the general's dog,' says the policeman thoughtfully. 'The general does not have dogs like that. His dogs are different.'

'Are you sure of that?'

'Yes, sir, quite sure.'

'I know it myself too. The general has high-priced dogs, but this—! He has neither hair nor shape. Why do people keep dogs like that? If such a dog should show itself in Petersburg or Moscow, do you know what would happen? They would not stop to look up the law but just—and that is the end! Khriukin, you have suffered pain, and I will not let this matter rest. I must give them a lesson!'

'But perhaps it is the general's dog after all,' the policeman thinks aloud. 'The other day I saw a dog like that in the general's yard.'

'Of course it is the general's' says a voice in the crowd.

'Yeldryn, help me put on my coat; it is cold. Take the dog to the general's and find out there. Say that I found him and sent him. And tell him not to let the dog out in the street. It is probably an expensive dog, and if every fellow hits him on the nose with a cigarette, he will soon be ruined. A dog is a delicate creature. And you, stupid fellow, put down your hand! It is not necessary to show that silly finger of yours. It is your own fault.'

'There is the general's cook. Let us ask him. Hello, Prokhor, come here a minute! Look, is that dog yours?'

'That dog? We never had such a dog in our lives!'

'He is not worth asking questions about,' says Achumyelof. 'He's a tramp dog. There is nothing more to be said. If I say he is a tramp dog, he *is* a tramp dog! He will be killed.'

'That is not ours,' continues Prokhor. 'That dog belongs to the general's brother, who has recently arrived. My master does not like that kind of dog, but his brother does.'

'So his brother, Vladimir Ivanovitch, has arrived?' asks Achumyelof, and a delighted smile spreads over his face. 'Well, well, and I did not know it! He is here on a visit?'

'Yes, sir, on a visit.'

'Well, well. So it is his dog, you say? I am very glad. Take him! A nice little dog. A quick little dog: he soon caught hold of the fellow's finger! Ha-ha-ha. Why are you trembling, you dear little thing? That man is a villain.' Prokhor calls the dog and walks away with him. The crowd laughs at Khriukin. 'I will catch you some day!' Achumyelof threatens him, and wrapping himself in his cloak, he continues on his way across the market-place.

The Hoop

FEODOR SOLOGUB

Feodor Sologub was the pen-name of Feodor Kuzmich Teternikov
(1863–1927), who was the son of a tailor and was born in St.
Petersburg (Leningrad). He published some poems and short
stories in 1897, but he also wrote long novels after the manner of
Dostoievsky. *The Hoop* is concerned with a poor old man who
once saw a rich child enjoying himself.

EARLY one morning, in a deserted street of a suburb, there
walked a lady and a boy of four. The boy was gay and rosy, the
lady was young and well-dressed. She smiled in her happiness and
looked anxiously at her son. The boy was bowling a hoop, a
large, new, yellow one. He ran after it laughing joyfully, showing
his bare knees and waving his stick. It was not at all necessary to
raise the stick so high, but that is what he did.

What joy! A short while ago he had no hoop, and now there it
was! And everything was jolly!

A shabbily-dressed old man, with coarse hands, stood at the
crossing and drew himself against the fence in order to let the
lady and her son pass. The old man looked at the boy with dim
eyes, smiling dully.

'A gentleman's son,' he thought slowly. 'A nice little fellow.
How he enjoys himself! A child—but a gentleman's child, of
course.'

There was something that he could not understand, something
that seemed strange to him. A child: but children are pulled by
the hair. They are in danger of being spoilt. And the mother did

not check her son. How well-dressed and beautiful she was! She evidently lived in peace and comfort.

When he—the old man—was a boy, he had led a dog's life. It was not too sweet even now, although he was no longer beaten or went hungry. In those days it was hunger, cold and blows. In those days there were no hoops or other such toys of the rich. His whole life had passed in poverty, care and bitterness. There was nothing to remember—not a single joy.

Smiling with his toothless mouth at the boy, he grew envious. He thought: 'A stupid amusement.' Envy made him weary. He went to his work—in a factory where he had worked from childhood, where he had grown old.

It was easy to remember the boy running and laughing, chasing his hoop. The whole day, amid the din of the factory machines, he thought of the boy and the hoop. And at night he dreamt of them.

Next morning he had dreams again. The machines rattled, the work was mechanical, and it was not necessary to think about it. The hands performed the accustomed task, the toothless mouth smiled at the dream. The air grew cloudy with dust; near the ceiling the belts moved smoothly from wheel to wheel. The far corners were noisy and dark. People moved about like ghosts: human speech was drowned in the noise of the machines.

And it seemed to the old man that he was a little boy, that his mother was a lady, that he had a hoop and stick with which he was playing, bowling the hoop with his stick. He was dressed in white and his knees were bare.

Day after day the same work and the same dream.

When returning home one evening, the old man saw in the street a hoop from an old barrel—a rough, dirty hoop. The old man trembled with joy, and tears came to his dim eyes. A sudden, almost unconscious desire entered his soul. He looked round cautiously, bent down, and with trembling hands seized the hoop and carried it home, smiling and ashamed.

He looked round cautiously.

89

No one saw him, no one asked questions. What business was it of anyone's? A little ragged old man carrying an old hoop of no use to anybody—who would notice him?

But he carried it secretly—in fear yet smiling. Why he had picked it up and why he was carrying it home he himself did not know. It was like the boy's toy, so he had taken it.

For several days the hoop lay under the old man's bed in his poor crowded corner. Sometimes he took it out and looked at it. The dirty grey hoop comforted him, and the ever-present dream of the happy boy became more real.

On a clear, warm morning, when the birds in the shelter of the town trees were singing more gaily than usual, the old man rose very early, took his hoop and walked out of the town.

Coughing, he made his way among the old trees and branches through the woods. He could not understand the silence of the dark trees. The scents were strange, the insects amazed him, and the dew was as in a fairy tale. There was neither din nor dust, and a wonderful soft darkness lay behind the trees.

The old man broke off a dry branch and put it through the hoop.

A field, bright and still, lay before him, and the dew shone on the newly-cut grass. Suddenly the man struck the hoop with his stick and set off at a run; the hoop rolled softly over the field. The old man laughed with joy and ran after the hoop like the boy. He threw out his legs, caught the hoop with his stick, and raised the stick high above his head as the boy had done.

It seemed to him that he was a little boy once more, gentle and happy. His mother was following him and watching him with a fond smile. Like a child he felt a little chilly at first in the dark wood on the gay grass.

The grey beard on the worn face shook, and laughter and coughs rushed out together from his toothless mouth.

The old man loved to come to the wood in the morning and

play with his hoop. Sometimes he feared that someone might see him and laugh; and at this thought an unbearable sense of shame possessed him. The shame was like fear; his legs grew weak under him. He looked round cautiously.

But no—no one saw him—no one heard him . . . And having played as much as he liked, he walked peacefully back to town, a light glad smile on his lips.

And so no one saw him, and nothing more happened. He played peacefully for several days, and one dewy morning he caught cold, took to his bed, and died. When he was dying in the factory hospital among strange people, he smiled serenely.

He was comforted by the thought that he, too, had been a child, and had laughed on the fresh grass under the shady trees while his dear mother looked on.

Boleslov

MAXIM GORKY

Maxim Gorky was the pen-name of Alexey Maximovich Peshkov (1868–1936), who was born at Nizhni-Novgorod. His father died when he was five, and the boy had to earn his own living when he was nine. For fifteen years he travelled widely in search of work, and when he was employed in the railway workshops at Tiflis he managed to get a story published in the local paper. This was the beginning of his road to fame. His longer and more ambitious plays and novels tried to find a solution to the problems of society in Russia.

Boleslov is a rather bitter love story.

THIS is what a friend of mine told me one day:

While I was studying at Moscow I lived in a little house where a strange girl was my neighbour. She was Polish; her name was Teresa. She was tall, strong, brown, with heavy eyebrows and vulgar features, as if cut with an axe. Her eyes looked dull, she had a deep voice, and her manners were those of a man who fights for a living. She was heavy in body and her whole appearance was fearfully ugly. We had opposite rooms at the top of the building. I never opened my door when I knew she was at home. Sometimes I met her on the stairs or in the yard, and she smiled at me with a bitter smile. Often I saw her coming home with red eyes, her hair in disorder. At such times she stared at me and said: 'Hullo, student!'

Her stupid laugh was disgusting. I would have changed my rooms to avoid meeting her; but the place was so pleasant, with the clear view over the city, and the street was so quiet, that I stayed.

One morning, after I had dressed and was lying on my bed, the door opened suddenly and Teresa appeared on the threshold.

'Hullo, student!' she said in her deep voice.

'What do you want?' I asked.

I looked at her. Her face wore an expression of confused shyness, something I had never noticed before.

'Student,' she said, 'I want to ask you a favour. Please don't refuse it!' I said nothing.

'I should like to write a letter home,' she continued.

'What on earth does she really want?' I thought. I jumped up from the bed, took a seat at the table, got paper and ink, and said, 'Come in; sit down and dictate.'

She entered, sat down cautiously and shot a keen look into my eyes.

'Well, to whom shall I write?' I asked.

'To Boleslov Kaschput, who lives at Swenziani, on the Warsaw Railroad.'

'What do you want me to write? Go ahead—'

'My dear Boles—my sweetheart—my love—my soul—may God protect you! My dear, why have you not written for so long a time to your little dove, Teresa, who feels so sad?'

I could hardly help laughing at her. This 'sad little dove' was almost six feet high, healthy, with strong fists, and a face as black as if the 'dove' had done nothing all its life but sweep chimneys!

But I kept my face straight and asked, 'Who is this Boleslov?'

'Boles, sir?' she repeated with astonishment, as if it was impossible that anyone should not know who Boleslov was. 'I am going to marry Boles—'

'Marry?'

'Why should you be so surprised, student? Can't a young girl like me have a sweetheart?'

'A young girl!' What a joke! 'Maybe,' I said. 'Everything is possible. How long have you been engaged?'

'For ten years.'

Well, I wrote a letter for her, so full of love and tenderness that I myself would have liked to be in Boleslov's place, if the message had come from anyone but Teresa.

'Thank you with all my heart, student,' said Teresa. She appeared deeply affected. 'Can I do something for you?'

'No, thanks.'

'I can mend your shirts and clothes, student.' That annoyed me somewhat, and I assured her briefly that I did not need her services. So she left.

Two weeks went by. One evening I was sitting at the window, whistling and wondering what I might do for amusement. It was terrible weather outside and I did not like to go out. Suddenly the door opened.

It was Teresa. 'Student,' she said, 'are you very busy just now?' Well, I would rather have seen somebody else.

'No. Why?'

'I wanted you to write another letter for me.'

'All right. To Boles?'

'No. I want his answer—'

'What!' I exclaimed.

'Excuse me, student. I'm stupid. I didn't express myself clearly. It is not for me, but for one of my friends—that is, one of my acquaintances. He does not know how to write. He has a sweetheart, like me.'

I glanced up at her. She looked ashamed. Her hands trembled and she was confused. I thought I understood.

'Listen, my girl,' I said. 'All that you tell me about yourself and Boleslov, and so on—all this is pure imagination. You were lying. It is only an excuse for coming here. I do not want to have anything to do with you any more; you understand?'

I saw that she was frightened. She blushed and tried hard to say something. I began to feel that I had misjudged her. There was something behind this; but what?

'Student—' she began; but with a sudden gesture she turned on her heel and went from the room.

I remained with an uneasy feeling in my heart. I heard her close her door with a bang. She was angry. I decided to call her back. I felt sorry for her and I would write the letter.

I went to her room. She sat at her table, her face in her hands.

'My girl,' I said, 'you—'

When I come to this point in my story, I always feel deeply touched. She jumped up, came straight to me with her eyes shining, put her arms on my shoulders, and sobbed as if her heart would break.

'What—difference—does it make to you—to—to—write— these few lines? Oh—you—looked like—such a good—fellow! Yes, there is no Boleslov—and—no—Teresa. There is only me— me alone!'

'What!' I said, astounded by her words. 'Then there is no Boles at all?'

'No.'

'And no Teresa?'

'No. That is, I am Teresa.'

I looked at her in astonishment. One of us was surely crazy. She went back to the table and brought out a piece of paper.

'Here,' she said, coming back to me. 'Here; take back this letter you wrote for me. You do not want to write a second one. Other people with kinder hearts will do it.'

She held in her hand the letter I had written for her to Boleslov. 'Listen, Teresa,' I said. 'What is all this? Why do you want other people to write letters for you when you haven't posted this one?'

'To whom should I post it?'

I gave it up. The only thing I could do was to go away. But she began again:

'No, he does not exist; there is no Boleslov. But *I want him to live*. I know I am not like others—I know what I am—but it does not harm anybody if I write to him.'

'What do you mean? To whom?'

'To Boleslov, of course.'

'But you say that there is no such person.'

'Oh, what do I care if there isn't! There *is* nobody, but I *imagine* that there is Boleslov. I write to him as if he were real, and he answers; I write again, and he answers again—'

At last I understood. I felt guilty, ashamed, with a shock like physical pain. Beside me lived a poor human being who had not a soul in the world to show her the least affection; no parents, no friends, nothing! And this poor creature had invented a man for herself!

She went on in her deep voice: 'This letter you wrote for me to Boleslov—I asked somebody else to read it aloud to me. I listened and imagined that Boleslov lived. And then I asked for a reply from Boles to his Teresa—to me. I feel almost sure that Boleslov lives—somewhere—I don't know where—and so I can manage to live. It is not so hard, so terrible, so lonely!'

Well, from that day on, twice a week regularly, I wrote letters from Teresa to Boles and from Boles to Teresa. I give you my word, they were full of passion, especially the replies. And she—she listened to the reading, sobbed, laughed, and was happy. In return she took care of my clothes, mended my shirts and socks, cleaned my shoes and brushed my hat.

Three months later she was arrested on some suspicion and put in prison. I have never seen her again. She must have died.

A Clump of Lilac

ALEXANDER KUPRIN

Alexander Ivanovich Kuprin (1870–1938) was an officer in the
Russian army, as the reader of this short story may easily believe.
He left the army in 1897 to devote himself to literature, and in
1903 his first book of short stories appeared. His novel, *The Duel*
(1905), made him famous, but in the Russian revolution he was not
a Bolshevik and he had to escape to France. His stories contain
more action than the usual Russian book, but his style has been
criticized as showing a lack of education.

NICOLAI YEVGRAFOVITCH ALMASOV scarcely waited till his
wife opened the door, and without removing his overcoat or
cap he strode into the study. As soon as his wife saw his gloomy
face with its heavy frown and the nervous biting of the lower lip,
she understood that a great misfortune had come upon him.

She followed her husband silently. In the study Almasov stood
for a while on the same spot gazing into a corner of the room.
Then he dropped the case that he held in his hand—it flew open
as it fell—and threw himself into a chair.

Almasov, a poor young officer, had just returned from the Staff
College. Today he had shown the professor the last and most
difficult piece of practical work: a local map.

Until now all his examinations had gone off happily and only
his wife knew the work that he had had to do. Even at the beginning his entrance into the college had seemed impossible at first.
For two years he had tried to get through the examinations, and

it was only at the third attempt that he had overcome all obstacles. Without his wife he would never have found enough energy and would have given up the attempt. But Verotchka helped to keep his spirits up. She had learnt to meet every failure with a clear, almost gay, countenance. She had gone without every luxury in order to surround him with the modest comfort which was necessary for a man who was doing brain work. She copied his papers, drew his plans, read for him, and was his notebook.

Five minutes of heavy silence passed. Almasov, without removing his coat or cap, sat turned to one side; Vera stood two paces away from him, also silent, with a look of suffering on her handsome face. She was the first to speak and she used that caution that only a woman can find at the sick-bed of a dear one.

'Kolya, was your work . . . unsatisfactory?'

He shrugged his shoulders and made no reply.

'Kolya, have they rejected your map? Tell me; don't mind. We can talk things over together.'

Almasov turned to his wife and began in that heated, irritated manner that people use when they tell of a feeling of injustice.

'Well, then, they rejected it, if you wish to know. To the devil with the whole business! All this rubbish'—he kicked the case containing the plans viciously—'all this rubbish may be thrown into the fire now! This is the end of college for me! In a month I shall be back in the regiment and in disgrace too. And all because of that cursed spot, too!'

'What spot, Kolya? I don't understand.' She sat down on the arm of his chair and put her arms round his neck. 'What spot?' she repeated.

'Oh, an ordinary spot of green. You know how I worked until three o'clock last night to get the map finished. The plan is well drawn and coloured: they all say that. Well, as I was sitting tired out last night, my hand trembled and I made a spot on it. Such a thick spot! I tried to rub it off and I made it worse. I sat thinking and wondering what to do, and then I thought I would draw a clump of bushes over the spot. It looked very fine when it was done; the spot was quite covered. I took it to the professor today.

' "Ah, yes," he said. "How did you get these bushes here, Ensign?"

'I should have told him there and then how it happened. He might only have laughed. But I don't really think he would have laughed: he's much too stiff and proper. I said to him, "But there is a clump of bushes there." "No," he replied; "I know the place as well as the palm of my own hand; there are no bushes there."

'A long discussion followed and there were a good many of our officers present. "If you are so sure of that clump," he said, "we must ride over tomorrow and inspect the place. I will show you that you were either very careless or drew the plan from a map . . ." '

'But why is he so sure that there is no clump of bushes there?' Vera asked.

'Oh, dear! What a childish question! Because for twenty years he has known that place better than his own bedroom, and because he knows his subject better than anyone else in the world. In the end they will all know that I lied.' As he spoke he kept breaking matches between his fingers, and when he had finished he threw the bits viciously on the floor.

Husband and wife sat thinking heavily without a word. Suddenly Verotchka jumped down from the chair. 'Listen, Kolya,' she said, 'we must go this minute! Get ready quickly.'

He frowned. 'Don't be absurd, Vera. Do you think I can go and apologize? Don't do anything foolish, please!'

'I don't want to do anything foolish,' Vera said, stamping her foot. 'I don't ask you to go and apologize; but if those stupid bushes are not there, we must go and plant some at once.'

'Plant? . . . Bushes? . . .' Almasov opened his eyes wide.

'Yes, plant them. If you told a lie, we must put it right. Get ready quickly. Give me my hat and coat—and my umbrella.'

While he was finding these things for her, Vera was quickly opening all the drawers of the tables, pulling out baskets and boxes, and emptying them on the floor. 'Ear-rings: only rubbish. They won't give anything for them. And this ring with its expensive stone . . . we must get it back again somehow. It would be a pity to lose it. Where is your cigar case, Kolya?'

In five minutes all her treasures were gathered together in her bag. 'Come along,' she said with a last look round.

'But where to?' Almasov protested. 'It is getting dark, and that place is five miles away.'

'Nonsense! Come along!'

They went first to the pawnbroker's. The man who valued their possessions was accustomed to the sight of human misfortune and examined their things calmly and for so long that Vera began to lose patience. He offered her three roubles for the diamond in her ring.

'It is a real stone,' Vera protested. 'It is worth thirty-seven roubles at least.'

The man closed his eyes with a look of weary indifference; but another of her treasures was valued highly, and altogether they managed to get about twenty-three roubles, which was more than enough.

When the Almasovs drove to the gardener's, the white St. Petersburg night was already spread over the sky. The gardener had just sat down to supper with his family and was very much astonished when the two visitors arrived.

He must have suspected some mystery, and to Vera's questions he answered, 'I am sorry, but I cannot send labourers so late at night and so far away. If tomorrow will do, I am at your service.'

There was only one thing to do, and that was to tell the

He offered her three roubles for the diamond in her ring.

gardener the whole story about the unlucky spot. He listened with disbelief, but when Vera reached the point when she thought of planting the bushes, he took more notice and smiled.

'Well, there is nothing else to be done,' he said when she had finished. 'What kind of bushes do you want to plant?'

They decided on a clump of lilac, and Almasov tried to persuade Vera to return home. But she was determined to accompany him, and she worried and hindered the gardeners all the time when the bushes were being planted. She only went home when she was quite sure that the grass round the bushes could not be distinguished from the rest of the grass.

On the following day Vera could not sit at home, but went out to meet her husband. When he was still some way off she noticed his vigorous walk and knew that the story of the bush had ended happily. And in fact, although Almasov was covered with dust and overcome with fatigue, his face shone with victory.

'It was fine!' he called out in answer to his wife's anxious look. 'Try and imagine how we got to the clump. He looked and looked and even tore a leaf off and bit it. "What kind of tree is this?" he asked. "I don't know, Your Excellency," I said. Then he turned to me and extended his hand. "I am sorry, Ensign. I must be getting old to have forgotten these bushes."

'He is a nice old man, and very clever. It seems a shame to have deceived him. He is one of our best professors. His knowledge is simply wonderful, and he is marvellous with maps and plans.'

But it was not enough to let Vera hear the story once. She made him tell her again and again, with every detail.

Almasov had never dined with such appetite as on that day. After dinner, when Vera went into her husband's study with a glass of tea, husband and wife burst out laughing at the same time and looked at each other.

'Why are you laughing?' Vera asked.

'And why are you?'

'Tell me first, and I'll tell you afterwards.'

'Oh, it was only nonsense. I was thinking about the lilac bush. And you?'

'I, too, was thinking of the lilac bush. Lilac will always be my favourite flower now.'

An Andalusian Duel

ESTÉBANEZ CALDERÓN

Serafín Estébanez Calderón (1801–67) was a Spanish writer and
professor of poetry and rhetoric at Granada. His descriptions of
Andalusian life and manners are famous, and one of the best of his
Andalusian Scenes (1847) is given below. He has been called one of
the fathers of the Spanish novel. Although the reader may expect
some violence in *The Duel*, he will discover that no blood is spilt.

THROUGH the little square of Saint Anna, towards a certain inn,
where you may drink the best wine in Seville, there walked
slowly two men. He who walked in the middle of the street,
taller than the other by about a finger's length, wore the hat of
Ecija, and his cloak was gathered under his left arm. His boots,
his strong appearance, his dark curly hair, his eye like a red-hot
coal showed that he was one of those men who can ride a horse
to its death and exhaust a bull.

His companion wore low shoes and many colours in his dress.
Rows of buttons ornamented his jacket. The open cloak, the hat
drawn over his ear, his short, clean steps, and the activity and
lightness of all his movements showed that he could laugh at the
most terrible bull or other beast.

I went slowly behind these great persons and, unable to prevent
myself, entered the same inn. But it was, in fact, an eating-house,
for there they serve food as well as wine, and as my readers see,
I like to call things by their proper names. I entered and sat down
at once but in such a manner that the two men did not notice me.

I saw that, as if believing themselves alone, they threw their arms round each other's necks, and thus began to speak:

'Pulpete,' said the taller one, 'now that we are going to meet each other, knife in hand, you here, I there . . . *one, two . . . on your guard, . . . have that, . . . take that, . . . and call it what you like* . . . let us first drink wine together.'

'Balbeja,' replied Pulpete, 'I am not the man to be vexed with such a friend as you. Let the wine be brought, and then we will sing; and afterwards blood—blood.'

The order was given and their glasses touched together. Looking at one another, they sang a Sevillian song.

This done, they threw off their cloaks with an easy grace and took out the knives with which to attack one another. Both blades were dazzling in their brightness and had been sharpened more than enough to cut stomachs open. The two men divided the air several times with these bright knives, their cloaks wound round the left arm, first drawing closer, then back, now more boldly and then in jumps. But then Pulpete raised the flag for discussion.

'Balbeja, my friend, I only beg you to do me the favour not to fan my face with your knife, because a cut might be so bad for it that my mother would not know me. And I should not like to be considered ugly. And it is not right for you to spoil what God made.'

'Agreed,' replied Balbeja. 'I will aim lower.'

'Except—except my stomach also, for I have always tried to be clean, and I should not like to see myself made dirty if your knife cut open my insides.'

'I will strike higher; but let us go on.'

'Take care of my chest; it was always weak.'

'Then just tell me, friend, *where* I am to touch you.'

'My dear Balbeja, there's always plenty of time and space to cut a man to bits. I have here on my left arm a black spot, and you can make meat of it as much as you like.'

'Here goes for it,' said Balbeja, and he hurled himself like an arrow. The other prevented the thrust with his cloak; and both, like skilful writers, began again tracing the letter S in the air, but without touching a particle of skin.

I do not know what might have been the end of this fight. I myself was not a suitable person to come between the two; and the innkeeper troubled so little about what was happening that he drowned the noise of their feet and of the falling furniture by playing a guitar as loudly as he could. Otherwise he was as calm as if he were entertaining two angels instead of two devils in the flesh.

I do not know, I repeat, what might have been the end; but another person entered to take a part in the drama. There entered, I say, a woman of twenty or twenty-two years of age, small in body but magnificent in boldness and grace. Neatly dressed and with clean shoes, she passed before my eyes with her arms on her hips and moving her head to and fro as she looked about her on all sides.

Upon seeing her, the innkeeper dropped his instrument, and I was overcome by emotions such as I had not experienced for thirty years. (I am, after all, only flesh and blood.) But without stopping to look at persons at the side, she advanced to the field of battle.

When Pulpete and Balbeja saw the lady Gorja appear, first cause of the fight and future prize for the winner, they increased their tricks, their curves in the air, their bending and their leaps—all, however, without touching a hair. For a long time our beautiful girl watched this historic scene in silence with that feminine pleasure which the daughters of men enjoy at such critical moments. But gradually her pretty face clouded over. Then she drew from her delicate ear, not a flower or ear-ring, but the stump of a cigar, and hurled it between the warriors. The effects were favourable. Both came forward immediately with proper respect; and each, by showing the disorder of himself and his clothes, recommended himself to the beauty in the splendid dress. She looked thoughtful, as if she was thinking over the fight. Then, with firmness and confidence, she spoke thus:

'And is this affair for me?'

'Who else should it be for?' they said in the same breath.

'Listen, gentlemen,' she said. 'Girls like me—daughter of La Gatusa, niece of La Mendez, and granddaughter of La Astrosa—know nothing of agreements; for they are worthless. When men fight each other, let the knife do its work and let the red blood flow. If you pretend you are fighting for me, it's a lie. You are wholly mistaken. I love neither of you. Mingalarios of Zafra is the man for me, and he and I look upon you with scorn. Goodbye, my braves; and, if you like, fight my man.'

She spoke, looking Pulpete and Balbeja full in the face. Then she went out with the same expressive movements with which she entered.

The two boasters followed the brave Gorja with their eyes; and then, with a shameful gesture, drew their knives across their sleeves as though wiping off the blood that there might have been. At one and the same time they put the knives away, and said together:

'It has never been known, nor do songs tell, nor do blind beggars sing, nor is it heard in the square or the market, that two courageous men killed each other for another's lover.'

'Give me your hand, Pulpete.'

'Your hand, Balbeja.'

They spoke and strode out into the street, the best friends in the world, leaving me amazed at the changeable nature of men.

The Stub-book

PEDRO DE ALARCON

Pedro de Alarcon (1833–91) came from Andalusia, which has
produced many of Spain's most attractive writers. At first he
studied law, but then he joined the army. He fought with bravery
and distinction, and won the San Fernando Cross. Later he took
to literature, and wrote plays, novels and poetry. His short stories
are still popular: for he can tell a tale well. *The Stub-book* is an
excellent example of the stories of the country and its people that
he liked to write.

OLD Buscabeatas's back began to curve during the period of
which I am going to tell, and the reason was that he was sixty
years old, forty of which had been spent working a piece of
ground on the banks of the River Costilla.

That year he had cultivated on his farm a crop of enormous
pumpkins, and these pumpkins had attained an orange colour
both inside and out, which showed that it was now the month of
June. Buscabeatas knew each one of them perfectly by its form,
its state of ripeness, and even by its name, especially the forty
which were fattest and richest in colour. He spent all his days
gazing at them tenderly, and sadly exclaiming, 'Soon we shall
have to part!'

One afternoon he decided on the sacrifice. He pointed to the
ripest of his beloved pumpkins, which had cost him so much
effort, and said the terrible words, 'Tomorrow I will cut these
forty and take them to the Cadiz market. Happy is the man who
will eat them!'

And he walked back to the house with slow steps, and spent the night with the agony of a father who is going to marry off his daughter on the following day. 'My poor dear pumpkins!' he sighed again and again, unable to fall asleep. But then he thought, 'What else can I do but sell them? I cultivated them for that purpose. At least I will receive fifteen *duros* for them.'

Imagine then his extreme astonishment, fury and desperation when, going the following morning to the farm, he discovered that he had been robbed during the night of his forty pumpkins. To save time I will merely say that he was filled with tragic fury and that he repeated again and again the terrible words, 'Oh, if I catch you, if I catch you!'

Then he began to reflect, coldly, and he decided that his beloved pumpkins could not be in Rota, his native village. It would be impossible to put them on sale there because they would be recognized. Besides, pumpkins fetched a very low price there.

'They are in Cadiz!' he decided after much thought. 'That rascal, the robber, robbed me last night at nine or ten o'clock and escaped with them at midnight in the cargo boat. I will take the boat this very morning for Cadiz, and I will be very much surprised if I do not catch the robber and recover the daughters of my labour.'

So saying, he yet remained about twenty minutes near the scene of the disaster, as if counting the missing pumpkins or planning terrible punishments for the robber, until it was eight o'clock and he left in the direction of the boat.

It was almost ready to sail. It leaves for Cadiz every morning at nine o'clock, carrying passengers, just as the cargo boat leaves every night at midnight, carrying fruit and vegetables.

That morning at half past ten Buscabeatas paused in front of a vegetable stall in the Cadiz market-place, and said to a bored policeman who was standing by, 'Those are my pumpkins. Arrest that man!' And he pointed to the merchant.

'Arrest me!' exclaimed the merchant, surprised and furious. 'Those pumpkins are mine. I bought them . . .'

'You'll be able to tell that to the judge,' answered Buscabeatas.

'I won't.'

'You will.'

'You're a rascal.'

'You're a thief.'

'You should speak with more politeness. Men should not talk to each other in this fashion,' the policeman said with extreme calm, hitting each of them in the chest.

Meanwhile a crowd had collected, and it was not long before there appeared the police inspector of the public market, the inspector of food.

The policeman told this great man what was happening. He questioned the merchant.

'From whom did you buy these pumpkins?' the inspector asked importantly.

'From Fulano, the old man from Rota,' the merchant replied.

'That would be the man!' cried Buscabeatas. 'That's the fellow I suspected! His farm is poor, and when it produces little he begins to rob his neighbours.'

'But if we admit that you were robbed last night of forty pumpkins,' said the inspector, 'how can we prove that these, and no others, are yours?'

'Why?' replied Buscabeatas. 'Because I know them as well as you know your daughters, if you have any. Don't you see that I have raised them? Look here! This one is called "the round one", that one is "the fat fellow", this one is "the red one", and that is "Manuela" because she resembles my youngest daughter.'

And the poor old man began to cry bitterly.

'All this is very good,' answered the inspector. 'But the law does not rest satisfied with the fact that you recognize your pumpkins. It is necessary that authority should be convinced that the thing already existed and that you should identify it with absolute proofs. Senores, you needn't smile. I am a lawyer.'

'Well, you will soon see the proofs that the pumpkins came from my farm; and you will see them without moving from this place.'

Buscabeatas's words astonished the spectators, but he dropped on the ground a package which he had been carrying in his hand. Then he knelt down and calmly began to untie the knots in the handkerchief which was round the package.

'What is he going to take out?' everybody asked with astonishment. At the same time another curious spectator joined the crowd, and seeing him, the merchant exclaimed:

'I am glad you are here, Fulano! This man says that these pumpkins, which you sold me last night, were stolen. You can explain . . .'

The newcomer turned yellow and tried to escape. But he was prevented, and in addition the inspector suggested that he should remain. 'I grew these pumpkins on my farm,' he said, 'and no one can prove the contrary.'

'Now you will see,' said Buscabeatas, opening the handkerchief. He scattered on the ground a quantity of pumpkin stalks, still green and fresh. Then, sitting on his feet and half dead with laughter, he said, 'Gentlemen, have you ever paid taxes? If so, have you seen that green book which the tax-collector carries. Receipts are cut from it, and they leave a stub by which it can be proved whether a receipt is false or not.'

'What you are talking about is the stub-book,' said the inspector gravely.

'That is what I am carrying with me; it is the stub-book of my garden. These are the stalks that were attached to my pumpkins before they were stolen from me. And if you do not believe me, look at them. This stalk belonged to this pumpkin. Nobody can doubt it. This other one, as you can easily see, belonged to this one. This one, which is wider, must belong to this other one. Exactly! And this one . . . and that one!'

As he said these words, he fitted a stalk to the hollow remaining in the pumpkin when it was plucked, and with astonishment the spectators saw that the stalk exactly fitted the shape of the hole. Then they all, including the policemen and the inspector himself, bent down low and began to assist Buscabeatas in this strange proof, all saying with childish pleasure, 'Yes, yes! It is certainly so! This one belongs here! Do you see?'

The old farmer's eyes filled with tears of happiness, and the policemen showed themselves ready to take the robber off to prison.

It is unnecessary to say that this pleasure was granted them, and that Fulano was obliged to return to the merchant the fifteen *duros* he had received.

Buscabeatas returned to Rota with deep satisfaction, but he kept saying on the way, 'How beautiful they looked in the market-place! I should have brought back *Manuela*, so that I might eat her tonight and keep the seeds.'

The Expression

JOSÉ FRANCÉS

José Francés was a capable nineteenth-century writer, many of
whose stories were concerned with women. *The Expression*, however, is of a different kind: for women play practically no part in
it. It describes the troubles of an actor who is not sure what expression of the face he must use at a certain point in his next play. At
the end of the story he is able to discover the right expression,
though in an extraordinary way.

THE manager of the theatre knocked at the door of Pablo
Heredia's dressing-room. 'May I come in?' he asked.

'Come in, Luis.' Heredia, the great actor, turned his gaze from
the looking-glass to the face of the manager. 'You look very
miserable, Luis. Small audience?'

'So small that we cannot go on like this, friend Heredia. We
must put on the other play, *La Fuerza rota*,★ as soon as possible.
Otherwise there will be no salaries next Monday.' He dropped
into one of the armchairs as he spoke.

Heredia did not answer, but turned again to the glass and
painted his eyes lightly. There was a long silence.

The manager put his trust in *La Fuerza rota*, a rough, brutal
drama dealing with crime, and suiting Heredia's temperament
exactly. The great actor had welcomed the work with enthusiasm,
and said that it would be his greatest triumph. But the final scene
worried him very much. In it the principal character receives a

★ The Broken Force.

113

knife-wound, and lies dying from loss of blood, unconscious at the feet of a woman.

During the rehearsals, Heredia gave only a suggestion of the proper expression of the face; but the manager and the author of the work saw there all the tragic intensity that the actor would show at the great moment when it came. They talked of it, and so did others in the theatre.

Heredia was proud at first; then shrugged his shoulders. Finally he began to experience an unreasoning dread of the third act. He was afraid of that expression in which he ought to show rage, pain, love and shame at defeat. What must the eyes be like? What colour ought the lips to acquire? How should the voice sound? Ought the hands to tremble? Should they have that weakness, that sickly softness that seems to stretch the fingers?

Cruel, terrible questions, to which he could find no answer before the looking-glass. They filled his thoughts during the day and kept him awake at night.

The rehearsals went on and on. The author and the manager fixed two or three dates for the first night of the play, and Heredia always postponed them. The news of his fear spread among the players and they made bitter jokes about the actor with that jealousy which is so common in the theatre. But in spite of the empty theatre, the author's despair, the manager's protests, and the fact that his reputation was in peril, Heredia refused to start the new play.

One evening the manager said, 'Well, friend Heredia, what are we going to do? I cannot go on like this. The author talks of withdrawing the piece. Think of it! We must fix a date.'

Heredia argued no more. 'All right. Say Monday.'

'Monday? Certainly not. Friday. Today is Tuesday. So in three days, the day after tomorrow, you will arrange the final rehearsal and I will tell the photographers. Do you agree?'

'Very well. I agree.'

About two o'clock in the morning Heredia left the theatre alone. The night was damp and misty. November was drawing to a close and the sharpness of the air made him turn up the collar of his coat.

He needed solitude, time to think away from the hot air of the theatre, free from the sudden anxiety that came to him because of the nearness of the first night—the first night that was going to make all their salaries safe.

He was dazed, doubtful, frightened, in that cruel state of mind when final decisions have to be made after long hesitation. How must he express those feelings in the last act? How ought the eyes to look? How should the voice sound?

As he walked along unconscious of the rain, he gradually left behind the broad central streets and came to the poorer quarters, which on that November night were wrapped in tragic darkness. Streets of crime and poverty, with lamps that shone yellow. He had been in such places before, searching for the types of people imagined by the author of this new play; but always with companions. Not as now, alone and full of anxiety.

Suddenly he stopped and looked around him. He had lost his way. He was at the far end of a narrow street. To the left, the blackness of some vacant land; to the right, tall and unfriendly houses with narrow doorways.

Not a voice; no sound of footsteps. He started walking back quickly, telling himself he was not afraid. Where could he be? He turned a corner and stopped to look at the new street. He did not recognize it, and continued walking through other streets, all unfamiliar. He grew more and more anxious and his mouth felt dry.

By chance he found himself outside an inn, and he remembered his search for the type of man in that last act. He opened the door, and the heavy evil-smelling air struck him in the face. The room was small and dirty. There were three tables occupied and one vacant. Behind the counter a fat man was reading a paper.

His entry caused considerable surprise. Then, when they saw him sit down and unbutton his fur coat, they whispered.

At one table sat an old woman taking short sips at a large glass of brandy. At another table a man and a woman talked in low tones. And at the last table, the one in the corner, were two men.

He ordered some beer and saw how foolish he had been to enter, to take off his gloves, and to let them see the jewels on his hands. So he acted boldly, and stared at the two men in the corner. They avoided his gaze. They were the type that goes to prison.

Little by little Heredia's fear changed into joy. The two men could be good models. Their foreheads were narrow, their eyes sunken, and the hairy hands had short fingers and bitten nails. The lower jaws projected with the expression of beasts. But in a short time, seeing that they were watched, they left.

Time passed. The old woman fell asleep on the table. Heredia got up, paid, and went out into the street. It was cold and misty as before and he looked up and down, wondering which direction to take. Well, it did not matter.

Long and narrow streets. His steps sounded on the pavements. Short and narrow streets. Suddenly a broad avenue with leafless trees and black factory-buildings at the end. He stopped and looked in vain for the two lights of a cab.

He heard footsteps behind him. He turned his head and thought he saw two men in the mist. Could they be . . .?

He continued walking, and suddenly two arms seized him from behind, a leg was thrust between his, and he fell sideways. Then a blow in the chest, a feeling of acute cold, and he lost consciousness.

When he opened his eyes they were laying him on a bed in an ambulance station. He felt a sharp pain in his left side. His throat was dry, his chest panting, his forehead damp. His nose felt strangely cold and he was very tired. Vaguely he remembered a knife-thrust. Perhaps death . . .

He also remembered the other thing, the expression which he had never expected to find. And suddenly, as if insane, he sat up in bed shouting, 'Here! Here! Quick! A mirror! A mirror! I want to see my face!'

The Rustic Cobbler

EUSEBIO BLASCO

The literary works of Eusebio Blasco (1844–1903) are very numerous and, if we include the plays, fill twenty-seven volumes. Many of them are light and amusing; but some of his work is bitter. *The Rustic Cobbler* is the kind of story which is very popular in Spain even today.

THE interested reader can apply this story to many circumstances of his life.

There was once a cobbler who lived shut up in his private boot-shop, that is, an attic in an Andalusian town. While he worked he saw the sun through the only window by which light came to the unhappy master of shoemaking.

This happened, as I said, in a city of the south, and the sun that bathes that fertile region only reached the poor cobbler in a single ray for a few hours.

Through the bars of his small window he saw the blue sky, and as he nailed or stretched his leather the poor man sighed with longing for some country unknown.

'What a lovely day for a walk!' he would often exclaim.

And when some customer brought him a dirty pair of boots belonging to the coachman opposite, the cobbler would ask him, 'Is it fine outside?'

'A splendid day! There has never been a finer April. Neither hot nor cold, and a gorgeous sun.'

The man sighed more deeply, seized the boots, and threw them savagely into a corner, saying, 'What luck you people have! Come back on Saturday for the boots.'

He tried to comfort himself by singing, and he repeated until night came:

> *He who would but cannot*
> *His liberty enjoy,*
> *Need have no fear of dying,*
> *For he's already dead!*

More longing looks at the heavens and more sighs, until sunset. The unhappy man was almost glad to see the darkness. His sad condition prevented him from enjoying the fresh air until evening.

One day a customer who lived in the same house came into his attic with a pair of country boots for him to repair. And as the cobbler with rustic ideas lamented that he could never see the country that he longed for, the other said to him:

'You are right, Gaspar. And therefore I say that the happiest people in the world are the donkey-drivers.'

'The donkey-drivers?'

'Yes. They come and go, always enjoying the fresh air, and smelling the flowers. They are the kings of the world. Yes, that is the finest work there is!'

When the customer had departed, Gaspar was thoughtful, very thoughtful. That night he did not sleep, but by dawn his mind was made up.

'Tomorrow I will tell my nephew to look after the shop, and with the fifty dollars I have saved I shall buy a donkey and become a driver.'

And so he did, and in eight days he was a carrier.

'What a lovely day! What healthy air! Now I'm living, and not wasting the best part of my life in that hole under the roof!'

And Gaspar, on his first journey, sang as he picked the flowers by the roadside.

There was not a soul within a mile. Gaspar was, as he had so often wished, in sole possession of the country.

Suddenly, as he rounded a corner, three men fell upon him, shouting, 'Halt there!'

One seized the donkey, mounted it, and started off hurriedly down the road. The next held Gaspar, while the third took what he had on him—money, clothes, everything! They left him naked and then, so that he would not run after them, gave him fifty strokes with a stick, till his ribs were black and blue. His shouts ought to have been heard in the capital, but no one heard them.

In broad daylight! At three in the afternoon in April!

Gaspar uttered terrible yells: 'Help! H-e-l-p! I'm d-y-i-n-g!'

At about five o'clock a farmer passed in a cart. He picked him up, wrapped him in a rug, took him back to the city, and put him down at the door of his house.

Great was the astonishment of his nephew and neighbours. Questions rained down on the beaten cobbler, but he answered none of them. He was not heard to say a word for many days.

But one day, about three o'clock, voices were heard on the stairs talking of a trip into the country: 'Let us go out for the afternoon.'

'What lovely weather! Tell our cousins to come with us!'

But Gaspar, alone in his attic, scornfully raised his head and looked at the sky: 'Lovely weather! What a thrashing those donkey-drivers will be getting!'

Three men fell upon him, shouting, 'Halt there!'

121

The Tomb of Ali-Bellus

VICENTE BLASCO IBAÑEZ

Vicente Blasco Ibañez (1867–1928) was better known as a novelist
than as a writer of short stories. *Blood and Sand*, one of his longer and
more ambitious books, was eagerly read by thousands. Although
his works were very popular when they first appeared, it is possible that most of them may soon be forgotten. Yet many of his
short stories, which appeared for the first time in the newspapers,
show a wealth of idea and invention which makes them good
reading.

AT that time (said the sculptor Garcia), in order to pay for my
daily bread, I passed a good part of my time restoring churches
and their stonework. I travelled a good deal doing this work.

Once I received an important commission: to restore the great
altar in the church of Bellus. While I and my companions were
busy on this, I sometimes sang something from *Aida* or *Faust*;
and possibly because of this, some of our neighbours came into
the church every afternoon: a lot of gossiping old women who
had nothing better to do than watch our work. Sometimes they
even criticized the colours we put on the stone. The best-looking
and probably the richest of them all, if I can judge from the
authority that she seemed to exercise over the others, sometimes
came up on the scaffolding fixed against the wall to show us how
important she was.

The floor of the church was composed of large flat pieces of
stone, and in the middle of it there was a large circular stone in
the centre of which was a rusty iron ring. One afternoon I was

122

standing on this stone and wondering what there might be beneath it. As I was stooping down and trying to lift the iron ring, the same woman—whose name, by the way, was Pascuala —came in and seemed to be extraordinarily astonished at seeing me in this position.

She spent the whole of that afternoon on the scaffolding, paying no attention to her companions below, but looking at me sharply as if she wanted to ask a question. Finally she asked it. She wanted to know what I was doing with that stone. In living memory no one had ever lifted it.

I denied having lifted it, but my denials seemed only to excite her curiosity the more. So, feeling a boyish desire to trick her, I arranged that every afternoon when she entered the church she found me standing on that stone and examining it closely.

We finished our work, took down the scaffolding, and prepared to leave the church. Just as I was about to go, the woman made another attempt to get at what she called my secret.

'If you tell me,' she said, 'I will keep the secret, Mr. Painter.'

And the painter—for that is what they called me—as he was young and full of mischief, whispered an absurd tale to her. I made her promise at least twenty-five times not to whisper a word of what I was about to say. I then told her a series of lies as fast as I could manufacture them. I told her I had lifted the stone by means of a mysterious force (of which I alone knew the secret). Beneath it I had seen the most extraordinary things. First I had found a long, steep staircase leading down into the earth. Then I had come upon a number of passages going in all directions. From one of them there came a faint light, and following this I came to a large room in which an ancient lamp was burning. It had been burning for a thousand years. In the centre of this room, lying on a marble bed, was a large man. He had a long grey beard, his eyes were closed, and beside him there was an enormous sword.

I went on to say that he was wrapped in a cloak that shone like gold and that he wore gold and diamonds in the cloth round his head. On the marble, I said, there were certain sentences in a strange language which even the priest himself could not read. But I was a painter, and painters know everything; so I had read it without the slightest difficulty. The meaning was—was—er—was—'Here lies Ali-Bellus. This tomb is dedicated to him by Sarah his wife and Macael his son.'

One month later, when I was in the city of Valencia, I found out what had occurred in that good little town after I had left it. Pascuala at once informed her husband, who the next day repeated the entire story at the inn. General amazement! They were astonished that they had lived all their lives in that town, had been to that church every Sunday, and did not know that just beneath their feet lay the great man with the long beard, the great sword, and the cloth on his head with gold and diamonds. And it was the great Ali-Bellus, who had a wife by the name of Sarah! And a son by the name of Macael! And he had undoubtedly founded the town! And all this had been seen by a stranger, who had been there only a few days, while not one of them had even suspected it!

The following Sunday, when the priest had left the little town to go and dine with one of his friends, a large part of the population rushed back to the church. The husband of Pascuala succeeded in getting the key; and all, even the mayor and his secretary, entered the church with heavy tools, iron bars and ropes. How they did sweat! That stone had certainly not been moved in three centuries. The strongest of them used every effort, but for an hour the stone did not move a fraction of an inch.

'Courage! Courage!' yelled Pascuala. 'Remember what is beneath the stone!'

Encouraged by her, they worked harder. In another hour they managed to pull up, not only the stone, but the greater part of

124

the floor of the church. One would have thought that the whole building was coming down, but little they cared about that! All looks were fixed on the hole before them. The boldest scratched their heads with indecision, but one, more courageous than the others, was finally lowered into the hole at the end of a rope. The rest held their breaths. That lowering did not tire them very much, because the man's feet reached the bottom even while his head was outside.

'What do you see?' they yelled together.

He was moving all round the pit, feeling with his hands and without finding anything but four solid walls and a few heaps of rotten straw.

'Look around! Search!' screamed those who had gathered at the edge of the hole; but he could find nothing but the four walls and the rotten straw. He climbed out, and others took his place, accusing the first one of being stupid. But finally all were convinced that there was nothing there but a hole about six feet square.

To say that they were angry would be to express it mildly. Their rage had no limits. The women took the opportunity to revenge themselves on Pascuala, who had made herself so important for years.

Their misfortunes reached their climax, however, when the priest returned. Seeing the floor of the church, and hearing the story of what had happened, he declared that he would close the church altogether, and was only calmed when the people promised to construct a better floor at their own expense.

'Did you ever go back there again?' one of those present asked the sculptor.

'Certainly not. More than once in Valencia I have met some of the inhabitants of this town and, strange to say, they seemed to think it was all a good joke. They all said that they were not among those who had gone into the church, for they had suspected the trick from the beginning. They always ended our conversation by inviting me to come and visit them. They smiled like angels when they gave me this invitation, but there was a certain look in their eyes which showed me that the town would probably be the unhealthiest place for me on earth.'

GLOSSARY

ABSURD: unreasonable; foolish.
ACADEMY: society for the advancement of literature, art, or science.
ACCURSED: cursed; evil.
ACUTE: sharp.
ADMIRAL: officer of the highest rank in the navy.
AGITATE: move violently; shake.
AGONY: extreme suffering.
AGREEABLE: pleasant.
ALCOHOL: strong drink; spirits.
ALTAR: holy table.
AMAZE: astonish; surprise very much.
AMBULANCE: small travelling hospital, usually in a car.
AMID: in the middle of.
ANONYMOUS: not having the author's name; of unknown authorship.
ANTIQUE: very old; old-fashioned.
APPETITE: desire for food.
APPROXIMATELY: about; not exactly.
APRON: cloth or leather worn in front to protect the clothes.
ARISTOCRACY: nobility; chief persons.
ARMCHAIR: chair with sides.
AROUSE: raise; stir up; awaken.
ASPIRIN: medicine which is supposed to cure headaches.
ASTOUND: astonish greatly.
ATTIC: room at the top of a house.
AUDIBLE: which can be heard.
AUTOBIOGRAPHY: life-story written by oneself.
AVENGE: take revenge for.

BACHELOR: unmarried man.
BALLAD: short poem which tells a story.
BANG: loud noise.
BASEMENT: lowest room of a building.
BEER: a strong drink.
BEWILDERMENT: puzzled confusion.
BISCUIT: hard dry bread in small pieces.
BLUSH: grow red in the face through shame or modesty.
BOARDING-HOUSE: house which provides food and lodging.
BOMB: container full of explosives.

127

Bony: thin and showing the bones.
Book: reserve; pay for in advance, so as to be sure to have.
Bored: very uninterested.
Bowl: send or roll forwards.
Brandy: strong drink made from wine.
Brigadier: army officer of high rank.
Brutal: rough and unfeeling.
Bullet: metal object which flies from a gun when it is fired.

Cab: taxi.
Café: coffee-house; place where one can have a light meal.
Cannon: big guns.
Canvas: rough cloth.
Cargo: goods which are carried by ship.
Ceiling: roof of a room.
Chameleon: small animal which can change its colour
Chat: talk idly.
Chocolate: a brown sweet.
Choke: stop the breathing.
Cigar: tube of tobacco, brown and rather large.
Cigarette: tube of paper full of fine tobacco.
Climax: top point.
Cloak: outer coat.
Clump: group of flowers or bushes.
Clumsy: heavy and awkward.
Clutching: feeling of being seized.
Coat-of-Arms: family sign; drawing which belongs to a family of high rank.
Cobbler: one who mends shoes.
Collapse: breakdown; a falling to ruin.
Comic: which causes laughter.
Comrade: companion; friend.
Concierge: person in charge of the entrance of a building.
Confirm: prove right; establish; assure.
Confiscate: take away as a punishment.
Corpse: dead body.
Cossacks: horse soldiers from north of the Black Sea, Russia.
Countenance: face.
Counter: long table (on which money may be counted).
Courtesy: politeness.
Crouch: bend down.

Dazed: puzzled; feeling stupid.
Dazzle: be bright; prevent from seeing clearly because of its brightness.

DECORATE: make beautiful or fine.
DEDICATE: devote completely.
DEFECT: fault; weak point.
DELICIOUS: good to eat or drink; pleasing to the senses.
DEMONSTRATION: expression of the feelings by marches, and so on.
DENSE: thick; with the parts very close together.
DEPRESSION: low state.
DEPRIVE ONESELF OF: take away from oneself.
DESPERATION: despair that leads to angry and careless behaviour.
DESPISE: scorn.
DESTINATION: place that one is trying to reach.
DETECTIVE STORY: story of a crime and of the resulting search (made by the police) for the criminal.
DICTATE: tell (someone) what to write.
DIN: noise.
DIS-: used before a word, this gives the opposite meaning. For example, *disobedience* is the opposite of *obedience.*
DISASTER: misfortune; terrible event.
DISGRACE: shame; dishonour.
DISQUIET: anxiety.
DISTINCTION: excellence.
DOVE: pigeon; loved one.
DRAMA: exciting play.
DRAMATIC: suitable for a drama; most interesting.
DRAWING-ROOM: sitting room; room to which the company goes after dinner.
DRIP: fall in drops.
DUEL: fight between two persons.
DUROS: coins; money.

ELBOW: joint where the arm bends in the middle.
ELOQUENT: having the power of smooth speech.
EMPHASIS: strong force in speech.
ENSIGN: the lowest rank of officers.
ENTHUSIASM: strong interest and liking.
ENTRY: coming in.
EXCELLENCY: a form of address for people of high rank.
EXHAUST: tire out; make very tired.
EXHIBIT: show.
EXQUISITE: excellent; of very fine quality.

FACE: that part of a mine where the earth is cut and the work done.
FANTASTIC: wild; almost unreal.
FATIGUE: tiredness.

FEMININE: womanly; of women and girls.
FERTILE: having rich soil.
FESTIVAL: feast; joyful meeting of the people.
FIST: closed hand.
FLEE: run away.
FOREFOOT: front foot.
FORSAKE: abandon.
FOX: wild animal of the dog kind.
FRACTION: small part.
FRANC: French coin.
FRO: from (only in the phrase *to and fro*).
FROWN: (i) angry look; (ii) look angry.

GALLOP: ride fast.
GAOL: prison (jail).
GASP: (verb) to speak, struggling for breath.
GEOGRAPHY: science which describes the surface of the earth.
GESTURE: movement of the hand or arm to show meaning.
GLARE: look fiercely.
GLIDE: go smoothly and easily.
GLOOMY: dark; sad.
GORGEOUS: splendid; very fine.
GOSSIP: talk idly; one who talks idly.
GROWL: make angry noises.
GRUMBLE: murmur with discontent; complain.
GUINEA: one pound, five pence.
GUITAR: musical stringed instrument played on with the fingers.
GULP: swallow.
GUSH: flow out violently.

HABITUAL: usual; customary; formed by habit.
HAIRDRESSER: one who cuts hair and arranges it.
HAUNT: come often into; visit often.
HEED: take notice of; pay attention to.
HEIR: one who receives property after its owner's death.
HEROINE: brave or famous woman.
HIND: back.
HIP: top of the leg.
HOARSE: rough in the voice.
HOOP: circle of wood or iron.
HORRIFY: fill with horror.
HURL: throw violently.

IDENTIFY: prove to be the same; show which it is.
IM-: not.
IN-: not.
INCREDIBLE: which cannot be believed.
INDIFFERENCE: lack of interest.
INDIFFERENT: not caring about.
INDIGNANT: surprised anger.
INEVITABLY: unavoidably; certainly.
INHERIT: receive property when its owner dies.
INSANE: mad.
INSOLENT: insulting.
INSPECT: examine; look at closely.
INSPECTOR: one who examines.
INTENSE: extreme; strongly felt.
INTENSITY: extreme force; strength.
INTERPRETER: one who explains the meaning.
IRRITABLY: with sudden anger.
IRRITATE: make angry.

JACKET: short coat.
JERK: (i) move suddenly; (ii) sudden movement.
JOLLY: happy; joyful.
JOURNALIST: one who writes for a newspaper.

LAMENT: say sadly.
LANCE: long pointed piece of wood or metal.
LANDING: level floor at the top of steps or stairs.
LANDLADY: woman who lets lodgings.
LASH: strike fiercely; whip.
LEISURE: free time; time without duties.
LICK: pass the tongue over.
LILAC: a pretty flowering bush with a pleasant scent.
LIME: a burning white solid. When mixed with water, it becomes very hot.
LIMP (adjective): not stiff; weak.
LIMP (verb): walk lamely; walk as if a leg is hurt.
LIVRE: old French money. Exact meaning is *pound*.
LONG FOR: want very much.
LOOP: circle.
LUGGAGE: bags and trunks for travelling.
LULL: make quiet or sleepy.
LUXURIOUSLY: richly; having more than is necessary.

MADEMOISELLE: title of an unmarried woman in France.
MAGICIAN: one who deals in magic.

MAGISTRATE: officer who deals out justice.
MASSIVE: big and heavy.
MISCHIEF: childish wickedness.
MISTY (adjective): Mist: cloudy drops in the air through which it is difficult to see.
MOAN: low sound of pain or grief.
MOISTEN: make damp.
MONSIEUR: title of a man in France.
MOOD: state of mind.
MOURNFUL: sorrowful; sad.
MUTTER (verb): to speak quietly without moving the lips.

NEGOTIATIONS: business discussions.
NEWCOMER: one who has lately arrived.
NOTIFY: tell officially; inform.

OBSTACLE: hindrance; anything that stands in the way.
OBSTINACY: firmness; refusal to agree.
OBSTINATE: refusing to agree; not ready to change one's mind.
OPERA: musical play.
ORCHARD: fruit garden.
ORDERLY: soldier who attends an officer, especially one who carries messages.

PANT: breathe hard and fast.
PAVEMENT: level stone surface of road or footpath.
PAWNBROKER: one who lends money if some article is left with him.
PEAK: top of a mountain.
PEN-NAME: name used by an author on his books or stories, when it is different from his own name.
PENETRATE: go through.
PENNILESS: very poor.
PERIL: danger.
PERIODICAL: magazine or other paper which appears regularly.
PERPETUALLY: continually; never stopping.
PHONE: telephone.
PICK: tool with a sharp point.
PLASTERER: one who covers walls with the white substance called plaster, which is made of sand and lime mixed with water.
PLUCK: pull up (a plant).
PLUNDER: seize the goods of another by force.
PORTER: man who carries bags for travellers.
PORTRAIT: picture of a person.
POSTPONE: delay until a later date.

PRECEDE: go before.
PROMOTE: raise the rank of.
PROP UP: support by putting something under.
PROSPEROUS: rich and successful.
PUMPKIN: large hard round fruit, sometimes cooked as a vegetable.

RAGGED: dressed in torn clothes.
RASCAL: dishonest fellow.
RATTLE: make a loud tapping noise, as when something is shaken.
RE-: again; back.
REBELLION: fighting against lawful authority.
REBUKE: blame in words.
RECKON: calculate.
RECONCILE: bring to contentment. RECONCILE ONESELF TO: make oneself accept.
REFUGE: place of safety.
REGIMENT: body or group of soldiers commanded by a colonel.
REGULATIONS: rules; laws.
REHEARSAL: practice of a play (before it is shown), so as to make the acting good.
REIN: long piece of leather with which a horse is controlled.
REJECT: refuse to accept.
RELIABLE: dependable; that may be depended on.
RELIEF: one who takes the place of another on duty in the army.
REMAINDER: what remains; the rest.
REPOSE: rest; quietness; stillness.
RESENT: dislike; consider as an insult.
RESOLUTE: very determined.
RESPECTABLE: not shameful; worthy of respect.
RESTRAINT: self-control.
RHETORIC: art of speaking and writing well.
RHEUMATISM: painful illness of the muscles and bones; it is usually found in damp countries.
RIGID: stiff; not easily bent.
RIOT: disturbance of the peace in a town.
ROLL: continued sound of a drum.
ROMANTIC: dreamy; liking the things that do not usually happen in real life but are wonderful and attractive.
ROSY: red and attractive in the face; having red cheeks.
ROUBLE: Russian coin.
ROUSE: awaken from sleep or sleepiness; stir up.
RUE: street (French).
RUMOUR: story which is heard but not certainly true.
RUSTIC: belonging to the country, not the town.

133

SALUTE: raise the hand to the cap as a sign of respect.

SCAFFOLDING: high platform on which workmen stand when they are working on the wall of a building.

SCULPTOR: one who cuts figures in stone.

SENSITIVE: having much feeling; easily affected.

SERENELY: calmly.

SERGEANT: a rank in the army or the police below the rank of officer; a sergeant wears three marks on his sleeve (the covering of the arm); each mark is in the shape of the letter V.

SHABBY: having a look of poverty; poor in appearance.

SHAFT: deep hole in the ground which is the entrance to a mine.

SHAWL: woollen cloth which covers the shoulders.

SHIVER: shake with cold.

SHRIEK: (i) sharp cry of fear or pain; (ii) cry in a high voice.

SHRUG: raise the shoulders.

SHUTTER: wooden or iron covering for a window.

SHY: modest.

SIP: drink in small quantities.

SIRE: title of address for a king or emperor.

SLAM: shut noisily and violently.

SLAP: strike sharply (as with the open hand).

SLEEVE: covering for the arm.

SLIPPER: loose shoe to be worn in the house.

SMASH: break in pieces violently.

SNIFF: draw breath in through the nose, so as to smell.

SOFA: long seat used in a sitting-room.

SOLITUDE: being alone.

SPECTATOR: one who watches.

SPHINX: creature with the head of a woman and the body of a lioness; it put questions to travellers and if they failed to find the answers killed them.

SPLENDOUR: noun of *splendid*.

STAB: wound with a pointed weapon.

STACK: pile.

STAFF COLLEGE: college for training officers who will assist the general or other commanding officer.

STAGE-COACH: coach which runs regularly with passengers from one place to another.

STAGGER: walk uncertainly and nearly fall.

STAIRCASE: group of stairs with wall at the side.

STALK: stem of a plant.

STALL: table on which articles are shown ready for sale.

STAMMER: speak with hesitation; hesitate in speech.

STARTLE: shock; frighten.

STRIDE: walk with long steps.

STUB: what is left when a tree is pulled down; what is left when a paper is torn off.
STUMBLE: catch the feet against something and nearly fall.
STUMP: what is left when a cigar is almost completely smoked.
SUBDUE: bring under control.
SUBTLE: fine and not easily understood.
SUBURB: outer district near a city.
SUSPEND: hang.
SWEETHEART: one who is loved above all others.

TEMPERAMENT: character and state of mind.
TENANT: lodger; one who lives in a place and pays rent for it.
TENSE: not restful; anxious.
TERRIFIC: terrible; very great and frightening.
TERRIFY: fill with terror.
THICKET: collection of trees or bushes close together.
THRASH: beat violently.
THRESHOLD: floor of the entrance to some place.
THUMP: heavy beating.
TILT: lower one end of.
TIMID: not bold; easily frightened.
TOMB: grave; burial place.
TORTURE: extreme pain.
TOUGHEN: make strong.
TRAGIC: very sorrowful.
TRAMP DOG: dog without a fixed home.
TRIUMPHANT: showing great joy because of success.

UNEASINESS: anxiety; not feeling at rest.
UNEASY: anxious.

VACANT: not occupied.
VAGUE: uncertain; without clear meaning.
VALUABLES: valuable things.
VEST: garment worn under the shirt.
VEX: annoy.
VICIOUSLY: savagely; fiercely; with extreme anger.
VIGOROUS: strong and active.
VILLAIN: man of bad character.
VIOLIN: musical instrument with four strings.
VISCOUNT: a title of nobility next below earl.
VULGAR: uneducated; rough; low.

WAG: move from side to side.

WALLET: case for the pocket.

WINDLASS: machine for raising heavy weights; when the handle is turned, the rope is pulled with great force.

WITHDRAW: pull away; take back.

WRATH: great anger.

YAWN: open the mouth wide when sleepy; an opening of the mouth when sleepy.

YELL: loud and sharp cry; to cry loudly and sharply.

ZOOLOGICAL: of animals.